DEBT 101

FROM **INTEREST RATES** AND **CREDIT SCORES** TO
STUDENT LOANS AND **DEBT PAYOFF STRATEGIES,** AN
ESSENTIAL PRIMER ON **MANAGING DEBT**

MICHELE CAGAN, CPA

Adams Media

New York   London   Toronto   Sydney   New Delhi

Adams Media
An Imprint of Simon & Schuster, Inc.
100 Technology Center Drive
Stoughton, MA 02072

First Adams Media hardcover edition February 2020

ADAMS MEDIA and colophon are trademarks of Simon & Schuster.

For information about special discounts for bulk purchases, please contact Simon & Schuster Special Sales at 1-866-506-1949 or business@simonandschuster.com.

The Simon & Schuster Speakers Bureau can bring authors to your live event.
For more information or to book an event contact the Simon & Schuster Speakers Bureau at 1-866-248-3049 or visit our website at www.simonspeakers.com.

Manufactured in the United States of America

4 2023

Library of Congress Cataloging-in-Publication Data
Names: Cagan, Michele, author.
Title: Debt 101 / Michele Cagan, CPA.
Description: First Adams Media hardcover edition. | Avon, Massachusetts: Adams Media, 2020.
Series: Adams 101.
Includes index.
Identifiers: LCCN 2019046051 | ISBN 9781507212660 (hc) | ISBN 9781507212677 (ebook)
Subjects: LCSH: Finance, Personal. | Debt. | Saving and investment.
Classification: LCC HG179 .C34 2020 | DDC 332.024/02--dc23
LC record available at https://lccn.loc.gov/2019046051

ISBN 978-1-5072-1266-0
ISBN 978-1-5072-1267-7 (ebook)

CONTENTS

INTRODUCTION

If you're like most people, the word "debt" can sound scary—but it doesn't have to. The truth is that debt will probably play an important part in your life, and as you'll discover, there are ways to use debt to your advantage. In this book, you'll find information about:

- The difference between "good debt" and "bad debt" and why, in some circumstances, it makes financial sense to borrow money and invest in your future (mortgages, student loans, and business loans, for example)
- What secured debt is and why it generally has lower interest rates than unsecured debt
- The best ways to make payments on different types of debt

Once you know more about debt, it will be easier for you to evaluate your own finances and figure out what to do about them. The information in this book will help you as you create a road map to financial security. *Debt 101* shows you how to design a personal path leading to that goal; along the way, you'll learn how to form a plan for dealing with different kinds of debt. Sometimes that plan includes cutting back on expenses and getting rid of drains on your finances. Other times, it means finding new income streams, such as side gigs; investing in rental properties; or other ways of bringing more money into your household. You'll be able to achieve financial security and freedom by understanding the best ways to borrow money, matching your expenses to your income, and saving for the future.

Dealing with debt head-on will help take anxiety out of your money management. You can get rid of the stress that comes with facing your monthly bills and build up savings to cover emergencies, goals (like buying a house or going on vacation), and retirement. The financial confidence that comes with understanding debt will help you overcome challenges that have been keeping you from getting ahead and accumulating a healthy nest egg.

To know when it's smart to take on good debt and how to rid yourself of bad debt—whether it's an excessively high mortgage payment, personal or payday loans, or credit cards—you need to set a clear course. *Debt 101* will help you get wherever you want to go.

Chapter 1

How Loans Work

A loan, at its most basic, is borrowed money that's expected to be paid back in the future with interest (extra money). Loans usually come with more rules and features than this simplified version, but at heart, they're just promises to return something.

Every loan has two sides: a lender and a borrower. The lender gives something, usually money, to the borrower. The borrower agrees to give back what she or he borrowed plus a bonus (whether that's extra money, an extra goat, or five days of labor) for the lender.

A BRIEF HISTORY OF DEBT

Ancient IOUs

Back before humans created money, they bartered to get everything they needed. Every trade was completed at once, and no one owed anything. As soon as the idea of currency came on the scene (long before actual currency appeared), all of that changed. The concepts of debt and credit began more than five thousand years ago, and they've continued to dominate the way people manage their money.

SHEEP AND SHELLS AND SHEAVES OF WHEAT

The idea of money showed up long before coins and paper currency. As far back as 9000 B.C.E., people all over the world used sheep and cows as cash. Some societies used cowrie shells, others used beads or feathers. People weren't out shopping with this "money," though. They were using it to settle disputes and arrange marriages.

Copper Coins

Metal coins first appeared between 600 and 500 B.C.E. when Chinese craftsmen created "cowrie shells" out of copper and bronze. Those shells soon evolved into coins, normally threaded on strings so they'd be easy to carry.

As societies solidified, merchants began to emerge. People began to purchase goods and services, with most purchases related in some way to farming. Very soon, customers fell into a buy now–pay later pattern, and the concepts of credit and debt were born.

Enter Debt

The first sign of debt appeared in 3500 B.C.E. in Mesopotamia. Various merchants recorded debts on clay tablets, confirmed by borrowers' personal seals. Merchants often used those debts as a form of currency to buy what they needed. Whoever ended up holding the ancient IOU got to collect the debt.

In about 1754 B.C.E., the Code of Hammurabi spelled out the rules regarding credit and debt. Instead of casual clay tablets, loans now required witnessed, written contracts. Loans now carried interest, and the code set strict interest rate caps (for example, interest on grain could not be more than 33 percent). Borrowers could pledge property to assure lenders that their debts would be paid. These early forms of collateral included:

- Land
- Houses
- Livestock
- Family members

When borrowers could not pay their debts, such as a farmer whose crops were wiped out in a flood, they often fled their homes. That became so common that kings sometimes offered general amnesty for debtors, giving land back to those borrowers who couldn't pay.

Ancient Credit Scores

By the time of ancient Rome, large amounts of money began to change hands and loans became part of everyday finances. That's partly because carting around several tons of coins was impractical, and it was easier to transfer ownership of the coins and buy on credit. People borrowed funds to bankroll trade, finance farms, buy properties, and invest. The loans were carefully tallied and tracked in account books held by both debtors and creditors; each entry was called a *nomen*, basically a name attached to an amount borrowed.

Those books also kept track of delinquent borrowers, protecting lenders from those likely to default. A farmer who was considered "untrustworthy," for example, would have a hard time finding a lender to finance his next crop. This practice was the forerunner of modern credit scores, which rate a borrower's ability and likelihood to pay off debt.

DEBT GETS BIGGER

International trade—meaning trade among nations rather than the earlier practice of trade within states—gained momentum during the 1500s. Individual countries developed more complicated financial systems to deal with the complexities of their economies and foreign trade.

National governments now needed to raise funds to finance expansion, trade, and wars. They turned to banks and then to the public to borrow money. Consumer borrowing began to expand as well, mainly through merchants extending credit to customers.

The First Modern Banks

Though technically banks have existed since the Roman Empire, the modern banks we're familiar with today appeared along with economic development. Giovanni de' Medici established the first bank in Italy in 1397. Other Italian banks cropped up, including the oldest bank still in existence today, Banca Monte dei Paschi di Siena, which has operated since 1472.

Banking systems spread slowly throughout Europe. In 1694, the British government formed the Bank of England to raise capital for its war with France. Nearly one hundred years later, in 1791, prompted by Alexander Hamilton, the Bank of the United States was established. That short-lived bank lost its charter in 1811 (it wasn't renewed by Congress), leaving the country without a central bank. The Second Bank of the United States had a similarly short run. It wasn't until 1913 that the nation would get a long-standing central bank, when President Hoover signed the Federal Reserve Act into law.

Consumer Debt Grows Like a Weed

For generations, people borrowed money to buy homes and bought goods from local merchants on credit. For many years, consumer debt was nothing to write about. But once the first universal credit card (Diners' Club) was introduced in 1950, consumer debt began to take on a different character. The first credit cards were actually charge cards, where any balance due had to be paid back immediately; you couldn't run a balance. By 1958, that changed when Bank of America introduced the first revolving credit cards (BankAmericard) in California. In less than ten years, that card went national, and people throughout the country began to build up credit card balances.

TERMS & CONDITIONS

Read the Fine Print

Because they're primarily written by big banks and lending institutions, loan agreements can be hard for borrowers to digest. They're full of terms and conditions that may be unfamiliar, especially for first-time borrowers. They're often very long and written in formal legal language (sort of like user agreements that most of us just scroll to the bottom of). Since these contracts affect your current and future finances, it's important to read and understand every word before you initial and sign them.

LOAN AGREEMENTS

Loan agreements are contracts that exist to protect both parties (the borrower and the lender) when someone borrows money. The contracts spell out exactly what the parties have agreed to and detail each party's responsibilities. They also detail what will happen if either party doesn't fulfill their obligations and how any disputes will be settled.

People are used to dealing with loan agreements when they borrow money from banks or mortgage companies, but not so much when loans get personal. In those cases, though, putting something in writing can protect both your finances and your relationships.

Different Kinds of Loan Agreements

There are many different kinds of loan agreements, and they range from super simple to dizzyingly complex. The simplest of these can be written in just a few words describing the arrangement between the borrower and lender ("I owe Joe $50," for example). The most complicated look like booklets, with dozens of pages detailing every facet of the loan.

Formal loan agreements are legally binding contracts between two (or more) parties. They typically cover fixed-payment loans, meaning the borrower has to pay the money back according to a schedule based on the terms specified in the agreement. They're normally added into public records, especially when the lender has the ability to seize the borrower's property (called collateral) if they don't pay the money back as spelled out in the contract.

The simplest loan agreements are called promissory notes. They include everything from an IOU tossed into a poker pot to a one-page fill-in-the-blank form with simple payment terms. Promissory notes serve as proof that one person owes another money and promises to repay the money. They may or may not contain specific time limits or payment amounts, but they do create a paper trail for the loan, though they don't offer the same legal protections as a formal agreement. These are often on-demand loans, which means that the lender can call for repayment whenever they want as long as they provide reasonable notice.

Put It in Writing

Loan agreements don't have to be written, but it's better when they are. That's especially true of loans made between friends (who want to stay friendly) or family members. Written agreements can prevent arguments down the line (such as disputes over how much was borrowed in the first place). They can serve as proof that the money was loaned rather than gifted. If there's interest involved, the agreement can include how the interest is calculated and what portion of each payment goes toward interest. Bottom line: Whenever you borrow or lend money, put something in writing to protect both sides.

UNDERSTANDING LOAN LINGO

Loan agreements contain a mix of financial and legal terms, and that combo can be confusing when you don't speak either language. Even some terms you might be familiar with, such as interest and principal, can come with unexpected twists in this setting. Lenders will throw these terms around during the loan process and expect that you understand them. Before you sign any loan agreement, get familiar with at least the most commonly used terms.

The Basics

Every loan agreement comes with four main features:

1. **Original loan balance:** the total dollar amount borrowed
2. **Interest:** a fee charged for the privilege of borrowing money, usually described as a percentage of the outstanding balance
3. **Loan term:** the length of time that the loan will be outstanding
4. **Payment:** the amount of money you'll return to the borrower periodically (usually monthly), calculated based on the loan balance, interest rate, and loan term

These four pillars form the foundation of the vast majority of loan agreements, but they don't look the same from one agreement to the next. Even if you're borrowing the same amount of money, the other terms may vary widely at different times and among different lenders.

Next-Level Lingo

Once you've conquered basic loan terminology, it's time for next-level language. You'll find these terms somewhere in most formal loan agreements, and it's important to know what they mean before you agree to them.

- **Annual percentage rate (APR):** the total charges you would pay (the cost of your loan) if you borrowed the full loan balance for an entire year, converted to a percentage and often used for comparative purposes
- **ACH payments:** letting your lender pull your monthly payments directly from your bank account
- **Collateral:** property that the lender can take and sell if the borrower doesn't pay the money back as required
- **Mandatory arbitration:** forces parties to resolve disputes privately through an arbitrator (a neutral judge) rather than through the court system; the arbitrator's ruling is final
- **Cosigner:** a person who promises to pay the loan if the primary borrower doesn't make the required payments
- **Amortization:** a series of fixed principal and interest payments used to pay down a loan over a stated period of time
- **Closing:** the meeting where money (and possibly property) legally changes hands
- **Prepayment penalties:** fees charged to discourage borrowers from paying off their debt early
- **Delinquency:** missing a single payment due date
- **Default:** not making a specific number (varies by lender) of consecutive payments, which can lead to serious financial consequences for the borrower, such as seized collateral and legal proceedings

You may come across other unfamiliar terms (or terms that don't mean quite what you thought they did) in your loan agreements. Before you sign, ask the lender to explain them to you so you know exactly what you're agreeing to.

The Difference Between APR and Interest Rate

APR and interest rate may look the same, but they're not. APR includes the total borrowing costs—interest *and* fees—that you'd pay over one year on the original loan amount, converted to an annual percentage. Interest rate includes just the percentage you'll pay periodically based on the outstanding loan balance.

AMORTIZATION

"Kill" Your Debt

Amortize, based in Latin, technically means "to kill." In loan lingo, it refers to "killing off" a loan by paying it down. Amortization is used for installment loans, where you make a specified payment (rather than choosing your payment like you can with credit cards, for example) every month. Over time, a portion of each payment reduces the principal balance of the loan, right on schedule.

HOW AMORTIZATION WORKS

Amortization is an accounting process that gradually reduces a loan over time with installment payments. Those payments are calculated using an amortization formula based on the loan balance, rate, and loan term. Each installment payment is split into principal and interest portions. While the total payments stay the same, the interest and principal portions change every time.

The balance of the loan decreases by the principal portion every month (or other payment period), though it may not seem like that at first. That's because with amortizing loans, the lion's share of early payments goes toward interest, with very little applied to principal. Over the life of the loan, that balance will shift, and toward the end, the interest portion will shrink to nothing.

Amortizing Loans

The big three loans—car loans, student loans, and mortgages—are amortizing loans. They all share specific characteristics, including:

- Equal installment payments
- Fixed interest rates
- Fixed payment schedule
- Fixed maturity (pay-off) date
- Consistently declining balance (not revolving)

Because of these fixed characteristics, you can see exactly how every payment will affect your debt as well as the total interest you'll pay over the life of the loan. That can be a useful tool for comparing loan options, such as loan terms (how long you'll borrow the money) and different interest rates. You may be surprised by how much more interest you'll pay over twenty or thirty years just because of a 0.25 percent rate difference.

Front-Loaded Interest

Every month (or alternate payment period), the interest portion of the payment is calculated by multiplying the current loan balance by one-twelfth of the interest rate. Since the balance decreases every month, the interest charge decreases as well. In the earlier years of the loan, interest will take up a much larger portion of the monthly payment. That's why amortizing loans are considered front-loaded: The vast majority of interest is paid in the beginning.

Mortgage Loans Didn't Always Amortize

Before the Great Depression, people borrowed only half the cost of their house, paid interest on the loan for five or ten years, and then paid back the loan in one lump when it came due, usually by refinancing. Once the Depression hit, housing values dropped and banks stopped refinancing, leading to a profound change in the mortgage loan industry: amortization.

AMORTIZATION SCHEDULES

With fixed-rate amortizing loans, you can see from day one the effect every payment (each one an amortizing payment) will have on your loan balance. An amortization schedule is a report of every payment to be made over the entire loan term and how that payment affects the loan balance. Many loan agreements include an amortization schedule among their exhibits, but you can figure it out even if you didn't get one from the lender.

Create Your Schedule

It's easy to create an amortization schedule for a fixed-rate, fixed-payment loan. There are dozens of online calculators available. If you prefer to DIY, you can use the template in Microsoft Excel, which has an extra column for (consistent) early payments. Basic amortization schedules include four columns (plus a date column):

- **Payments:** your regular monthly payment that includes principal and interest but not taxes and insurance
- **Interest expense:** the portion of the current payment going toward interest, calculated by multiplying last month's ending loan balance by the monthly interest rate (annual rate divided by twelve)
- **Principal:** the principal portion of the payment, calculated by subtracting the current interest from the full payment
- **Balance:** the remaining loan balance (ending balance) after subtracting this month's principal payment

Your amortization schedule may also include cumulative interest, which is a running total of the interest paid each month so you can see how much interest you're paying over time. Some schedules include a column for extra payments, which get applied directly to principal.

For Variable-Rate or Revolving Loans

Creating an amortization schedule for a loan with a variable interest rate or for a revolving loan (like a line of credit or a credit card) is much tougher, as these don't fit neatly into the amortizing loan category. Since you can't accurately predict how rates and payments will change with variable-rate loans, you won't be able to create a true amortization schedule for your loan. What you can do is come up with different assumptions to see how they might affect your repayment schedule.

With revolving loans, the principal amount goes up (with more borrowing) and down (with payments), which also makes it harder to create an accurate amortization schedule. It is possible with a home equity line of credit where you borrow more money only occasionally, but virtually impossible with an active credit card. (Don't even bother trying with a revolving, variable-rate loan; you'll just end up frustrated for no reason.) You can find revolving loan amortization calculators and variable-rate amortization calculators online at www.bankrate.com or www.mortgagecalculator.org. Remember, these will be best guesses and may be way off from your actual future amortization schedule.

DIFFERENT TYPES OF DEBT

Name That Debt

Debt comes in many different forms, but most of those fit neatly into big-picture categories. The main categories involve security and totality. Security here refers to the lender's security and how they can get their money back if you don't pay. Totality speaks to whether the amount you borrow remains fixed or changes (meaning you can borrow more money on the same loan). Both factors impact the interest rate attached to the loan.

SECURED VERSUS UNSECURED

One key to categorizing debt is based on what's behind the debt, backing it up. Debt can be either secured or unsecured depending on whether or not the lender has a claim on some sort of property. That distinction can have a great effect on interest rates, as it speaks to the lender's overall risk in lending the money.

From a borrower's perspective, paying secured debts takes top priority when there's not enough money to pay every bill. Though these payments often take up more of the available budget, you stand to lose crucial assets (like your home or your car) if these debts are not paid regularly.

Secured Debt

Secured loans are backed by some form of collateral, which is property (like a car or a house) pledged to satisfy the debt if the loan is not paid. With this kind of loan, the lender will place a lien (a claim on an asset) on the collateral that allows them to take it if the borrower doesn't pay. For example, the lender could repossess a car or foreclose on a house.

The collateral doesn't have to have any relation to the loan, though it usually does. For example, a car loan usually comes with a lien on that car. Collateral can be pledged to secure loans not tied to any particular asset (for example, some personal loans may require collateral). Because of the built-in safety net, secured loans (from reputable lenders) typically come with lower interest rates.

Creative Collateral

"Collateral" usually refers to things like cars, houses, and investment securities, but they're not limited to these assets. As long as the lender agrees, anything of value can work. Some more creative choices include designer handbags, wheels of Parmesan cheese, thoroughbred horses, and star soccer players (on Real Madrid).

Unsecured Debt

Unsecured debt doesn't come with the security of collateral. Here, the lender is banking on your ability and willingness to make all of the scheduled payments.

Examples of unsecured debt include:

- Student loans
- Credit card debt
- Personal loans
- Medical bills

Technically, payday loans fall into the unsecured debt category, but this isn't exactly correct. While there's no physical collateral (like a car or a house) pledged to the payday lender, borrowers do have to provide direct access (through a post-dated check or an ACH withdrawal, for example) to their paychecks when they arrive.

REVOLVING VERSUS NONREVOLVING

Revolving and nonrevolving describe the way money is borrowed. Revolving debt allows you to borrow money at will, up to a preset limit, and then borrow that money again as often as you like. Nonrevolving debt refers to a one-time loan for a fixed dollar amount, and once it's repaid, you can only borrow again by applying for a new loan.

Revolving debt makes up about 25 percent of the total outstanding US consumer debt in dollars (as of May 2019, according to the Federal Reserve). That's because individual nonrevolving loans tend to be bigger, covering big-ticket items like mortgages, student loans, and car loans.

Revolving Debt

With revolving loans, such as home equity lines of credit (HELOCs) and credit cards, your balance due goes up and down depending on your financial activity. You can borrow more at will, up to your limit, and your monthly payment amount can vary based on the current outstanding debt.

Revolving debt is sometimes referred to as open-ended debt, because you can borrow the same money repeatedly. As you make payments, your available credit increases; as you borrow more, your available credit decreases. Even though you can only borrow up to the maximum credit limit at any given time, you can borrow much more than that over time. Revolving debt can be secured, such as a HELOC secured by your home, or unsecured, such as credit card debt.

Nonrevolving Debt

With a nonrevolving loan, you borrow a set amount of money in one shot, and the lender expects to be paid back according to a schedule. These loans are predictable, come with planned payments, and have predetermined payoff dates. Both parties know from the start when the loan will be paid in full. If you need more money, you have to start the process again from the top and take out another loan. Examples of nonrevolving debt include car loans and mortgages.

In most circumstances, the outstanding balance of a nonrevolving loan will only decline over time. (The exception is a loan with negative amortization, when unpaid interest gets added to the balance of the loan.) Nonrevolving debt can be either secured or unsecured.

PREDATORY LENDING

Legal Loan Sharks

Predatory lenders take advantage of desperate or uninformed borrowers. While these lenders often pretend that they're helping you, their only goal is maximizing their profits by lending you as much money as possible at the highest interest rate possible. They don't care if the debt is too much for you to manage based on your current financial situation. In fact, they often specifically target people who can't really afford the loans. Those borrowers often end up trapped in a dangerous debt cycle with thoroughly trashed credit. Many end up losing their homes.

While it seems like predatory lending should be illegal, it isn't always. The federal government offers some protections, and twenty-five states have specific anti–predatory lending laws. But many lenders work through loopholes, and others just flat-out break the law. You have to protect yourself and your finances by knowing the signs and walking away, even if you're desperate for a loan. Your situation will certainly get even worse if you borrow from a predatory lender.

SIGNS OF A PREDATORY LENDER

There's no standard definition for predatory lending, so learning what to watch out for can help you avoid these unscrupulous practices. Some of these are harder to spot than others, so you have to be very cautious. If you notice any of these red flags, you are dealing with a predatory lending practice, and you should stop the process immediately.

- **Surprisingly good offer.** Predatory lenders reel you in with the promise of plenty of quick cash, lower-than-market interest rates, and instant money regardless of how bad your credit score is (and sometimes even if you're unemployed). If a deal sounds too good to be true, read every single word of the fine print, and you'll see that it's not.

- **No credit check.** Reputable lenders will always check your credit. Predatory lenders don't care, because they've built in ways to get their money back (through outrageously high interest or by tricking you into putting up collateral, for example).

- **Blank spaces.** If a lender expects you to sign a loan contract with *any* (even one) blank spaces in it, do not sign it. I can't stress this enough: *Never sign a contract with blank spaces.*

- **Excessive fees.** Predators charge dramatically higher fees for common loan costs (like document prep fees) than reputable lenders do. If the fees are out of line with your research, walk out.

- **Pressure.** Predatory lenders will pressure you and play on your fears and insecurities to get you to borrow from them. If you feel pressured to sign when you're not ready or comfortable, leave.

- **False or incomplete disclosure.** Predatory lenders lie or hide information about the loan. If you can't easily tell how much the loan will cost you, don't take it.

- **Mandatory electronic payments.** If giving the lender access to your bank account is the only available form of payment, leave. Reputable lenders will offer you that as an option, usually in exchange for reduced fees or interest rate. Predatory lenders require this so they can request payment repeatedly until it goes through, which can leave you on the hook for multiple overdraft fees.

- **Vague answers.** Reputable lenders help make sure you understand everything in the loan documents and will clearly answer all of your questions. Predatory lenders won't give you straight answers and may "reassure" you that they're taking care of everything so you don't have to worry. If your questions get vague (or no) answers, don't sign.

Predatory lenders know you're in a tight spot; that's why they're talking to you. They're hoping that you're so desperate for money you'll just sign anything they put in front of you. They promise an "easy way out" of your financial hardship, but that promise is a lie. With predatory lending practices, your financial situation will only get worse.

HOW TO PROTECT YOURSELF FROM PREDATORY LENDERS

The best way to avoid predatory lenders is to look for reputable lenders. Trustworthy lenders will look at your credit and financial situation to make sure you can reasonably expect to pay back the money you're borrowing. They will try to work with you and walk you through the process.

To be clear, just because something comes with a high interest rate doesn't mean the lender is predatory. If you have bad credit, a lot of debt relative to your income, or other signs that make lending to you risky, you should expect to pay higher-than-average interest rates—just not abusively high rates. If you have any doubts at all about a lender, take a step back and do some checking.

Do Your Homework

Before you work with an unfamiliar lender, take the time to check them out. A few simple online searches will tell you everything you need to know. First stop: complaints and bad reviews. While even reputable lenders will have some of both, predatory lenders will usually have floods of complaints and bad reviews. Next, check whether the lender is registered to offer loans in your state; if the company website doesn't list the states where it legally conducts business, it's not legit. You'll also want to make sure that the lender has a physical address (not just a website or a PO Box) and verify that the address is real. If all of that checks out, still visit the Better Business Bureau (www.bbb.org) and your state attorney general's office (www.naag.org).

Fight Back

If you're stuck with a predatory loan, you can fight it. Report the lender to the Federal Trade Commission (FTC) (www.ftc.gov). Talk with a lawyer to see if you can escape the loan or sue the lender under the Truth in Lending Act (TILA). There are protections available, but you have to activate them.

Find Safer Ways to Get the Money

If your situation is so bleak that you can't borrow from traditional lenders, you have options other than turning to a predatory lender. Some of these alternatives may make you uncomfortable, and that's hard to work through. But, honestly, the outcome will be better in the long run.

Other options include:

- Get an advance on your paycheck either directly from your employer or through an app like Branch or Chime.
- Get a payday alternative loan (PAL) from your credit union (if you don't belong to a federal credit union, join one), as these loans are designed to help you pay them back.
- Borrow money from family or friends, but do it the right way with a signed note and a specific payback schedule that you can (and will) follow.
- Get government assistance to help you pay bills and make ends meet; start with the Benefit Finder at www.benefits.gov for federal aid and the Community Action Partnership (CAP) at https://communityactionpartnership.com for local aid options.
- Talk to your creditors and explain your situation; if you contact them (the earlier the better), they may help you work out a temporary reduced payment plan or even let you temporarily suspend payments until you're able to get back on track.

A combination of these options can keep you away from the usually permanent financial damage caused by predatory loans. It can be stomachache-causing hard to ask for this kind of help, but it will protect you from losing your car or your home or your financial future to a predatory lender.

Chapter 2

The Right Way to Borrow Money

The best time to borrow money is when you don't need to do it, but choose to do it. When you're financially stable with great credit and a high net worth (especially if you have a lot of liquid assets, which can be quickly converted to cash), lenders will trip over themselves to offer you loans. That means you'll be in the strongest possible position to negotiate terms that benefit you, mainly very low interest rates.

Since you don't need to borrow money to cover your expenses, you'll use loans for leverage to build up your wealth more quickly. That involves using other people's money to purchase productive assets, which will either produce steady income or come with the potential to grow significantly in value.

BORROWING VERSUS DEBT

Good Debt/Bad Debt

When it comes to debt, the type makes a big difference. Good debt goes toward building your net worth by investing in assets (including yourself); the goal of this debt is to increase your fortune or your fortune-growing ability. Bad debt eats away at your net worth and jeopardizes your current and future financial health. This type of debt is used to buy things that won't add value to your nest egg or boost your income. Some debt falls into the middle (like car loans) and doesn't fit neatly into either the good or bad category.

Understanding the differences can help you make better borrowing choices. But don't beat yourself up over bad debt; you can't always avoid it. In fact, it's nearly impossible for most people to get by without racking up at least a little bit of bad debt. The key is to minimize it and pay it off as quickly as possible, before it takes over your finances completely.

GOOD DEBT

Good debt works for you, helping achieve goals, boost income, and improve your overall financial situation. This type of debt normally comes with lower interest rates and better payment terms, which is also better for your net worth.

Still, too much good debt is bad for your finances. That's why it's important to not take on more debt than you can realistically pay back without straining your budget. This is especially true of student loans, which many young people enter into without fully realizing the long-term (sometimes devastating) financial implications.

Student Loans

Borrowing to fund your education falls into the good debt category; it's an investment in yourself and your future. Choosing the right degree program plays a crucial role in this conversation. When your education will be funded (even partly) by loans, the degree has to lead to the possibility of an income-producing career path, or the debt could quickly become unmanageable.

The dividing line that keeps student debt in the good category involves the amount you borrow. While most people look at the question as "How much in student loans *can I get*?" the right question is "How much in student loans *can I pay back*?" To keep these loans affordable, the rule of thumb is to borrow (in total) no more than your (realistically) expected starting salary when you graduate, and less is even better.

We Owe Trillions

Mortgages remain by far the largest piece of household debt in the US. According to the Federal Reserve, consumer mortgage debt hit $9.4 trillion (as of June 2019), a record-breaking high. Total household debt for the period was $13.86 trillion.

Home Mortgage Loans

Your mortgage will probably be the single largest good debt you ever take on. These loans offer the most direct path to owning a home, both a functional and usually appreciating (growing in value) asset. As these loans run hundreds of thousands of dollars, it's important to fully understand how the loan terms and the interest rate will affect your current and future financial picture. Go into these loans knowing how much of a monthly payment fits easily into your budget and avoid the temptation to go bigger.

Small Business Loans

Funding a business opens the possibility for a more secure financial future, where your financial success is limited mainly by your own determination and motivation. With a lot of drive and some luck, you'll be able to turn your business into a reliable income stream for your family and a source of retirement funding when you're ready to stop. The key to keeping this type of loan in the good pile is starting with a complete business plan, whether you're in prelaunch or expansion mode. Know exactly how you'll use the money to expand your company and your chances of success improve instantly.

BAD DEBT

Borrowing money to pay for discretionary expenses (things you want but don't really need) counts as bad debt. High-interest debt also belongs here, even if it's used for needs, because it will make whatever you use it for two or three times more expensive than if you'd paid for it outright. That can trap you in a cycle of relying on loans to cover your basic monthly expenses that can be extremely hard to escape.

Credit Card Debt

Using credit cards and having credit card debt are not the same thing. Credit card debt involves a balance due that can't be cleared with a single payment. This tops the list of bad debt for three important reasons:

1. High interest rates
2. Payment schedules designed to keep you in debt
3. Often used to buy consumables, services, and goods that immediately lose value

Paying off this debt will lead to a huge improvement in your immediate financial situation, your long-term financial security, and your net worth.

Personal Loans

Taking out personal loans to buy big-ticket items like a new wardrobe or a vacation counts as bad debt. This form of unsecured debt normally comes with fairly high interest rates (sometimes as high as credit card rates), adding an extra layer of cost to the purchase, especially if you don't make consistent, on-time loan payments. In addition, you may have to cough up money for fees (like loan origination fees) on top of the loan interest.

In specific cases, personal loans can move to the medium debt category. Using a lower-high-interest personal loan to pay off higher-interest debt (like payday loans) would be a better use of this type of debt.

Payday Loans

Payday loans fall into the toxic debt category, as they come with frighteningly high interest rates—some as high as 500 percent a year—and are virtually impossible to pay back. The goal of payday lenders is to keep you borrowing constantly; it's how they make money. These short-term loans are supposed to keep you afloat until your next paycheck, but borrowing even a small amount at these unconscionable rates can cost a fortune. For example, a single $500 payday loan could come with a $75 fee, which converts to 15 percent interest for two weeks. That comes out to an annual interest rate of 360 percent, ten times more than the highest-rate credit cards.

Worse, you have to pay that loan back with your next paycheck, even if you need that money to pay for your living expenses like rent and food. That forces you to take out another payday loan over and over again. If you have any options other than a payday loan—even a super high-interest credit card cash advance—use them. These toxic loans are the worst kind of bad debt.

MEDIUM DEBT

This middle zone of debt covers everything that doesn't fall squarely into either the good debt or bad debt category. This debt covers things that you absolutely need, even if you can't afford to pay for them in full with cash.

Debts that fall into the medium category include:

- **Car loans.** If you need a car to get around, which many of us do, you may have to borrow money to get one. To keep this medium debt from turning into bad debt, stick with good quality, afford-able used cars; keep the loan term to four years or less; and shop around for rates before you sign up for seller financing.
- **Medical debt.** No matter your financial situation, protecting your and your family's physical and mental health is worth any cost, even if that includes taking on debt. Many healthcare providers will negotiate balances or provide you no-interest payment plans, a key reason to *not* pay for medical expenses with credit cards.

CREDIT BUILDING COMES FIRST

Prove You'll Pay

Most people don't think about their credit scores until either they're ready to buy a house or they've been declined for a credit card or loan. That's a mistake, as credit reputation has become an increasingly important part of life, affecting much more than just borrowing money.

Building strong credit will improve your financial life from the time you get your first credit card and help you use debt to your advantage. Paying attention to your credit can help you develop better financial habits, which will serve your net worth and your future fortune.

ESTABLISH YOUR CREDIT

There are many reasons to establish good credit, but the main one is saving money. With a positive credit history and a strong credit score, you can save thousands of dollars every time you borrow money in the form of lower interest rates. Lower interest rates mean smaller, more budget-friendly loan payments, plus less of your money goes to the bank (or mortgage lender or credit card issuer).

Credit Affects More Than You Think

Whether you're thinking about borrowing money or not, it's important to establish credit and maintain a good credit score. Most people don't realize that your credit score can impact other areas of your life as well, such as:

- Renting an apartment
- Getting a job
- Getting life insurance
- The amount you pay for auto insurance
- Whether you have to pay a utility company deposit

Plus, when (if) you are ready to borrow some money, having a top credit score makes you eligible for the lowest interest rates and the best loan terms. That can make your borrowing a more effective part of your overall financial plan.

Meet FICO and the Bureaus

Generally, when people are talking about credit scores, they're talking about FICO (named after the Fair Isaac Corporation), which is the most widely used credit scoring system in the US. The three major credit-reporting bureaus each put their own spin on the FICO score and mix that with information they collect from lenders (otherwise there'd be no need for three of them). Those three credit bureaus are Equifax, Experian, and TransUnion.

Credit scores typically range from 300 to 850, and bigger is better. Your score is based on five main components (in order of weight):

1. Payment history (whether you pay on time and in full)
2. Credit utilization (how much you owe compared to available credit)
3. Length of credit history
4. Credit mix (the different types of debt you have, for example, credit cards and a mortgage)
5. New credit (how much new credit you've applied for based on new inquiries)

Different lenders have slightly different guidelines when it comes to credit scores, but generally consider scores higher than 700 to be good, scores above 750 to be very good, and scores over 800 to be excellent.

Join the 800+ Club

More Americans than ever before have top-tier credit scores. According to Investopedia, 21.8 percent of us landed in the 800–850 range (in 2018, the most recent data available). In real terms, that means better interest rates, better loan terms, and better rewards on credit cards.

How to Establish Credit When You Don't Have Any

It seems like a catch-22: You can't establish credit without borrowing, but you can't borrow if you haven't established credit. Luckily, there are simple tools you can use to get your credit history rolling (no matter how old you are).

On the credit card front, you have two choices: become an authorized user on someone else's card or get your own secured credit card. If you have a willing family member or friend with stellar credit, ask them to make you an authorized user. Their credit helps build your credit as long as the card issuer reports all authorized users to the credit bureaus. Alternately, you can get a secured credit card, which works like a regular credit card with a cash safety net. Basically, you supply a cash deposit (the secured part) to cover your credit limit, then use the card and make on-time monthly payments.

You can also use similar tools to take out loans. For credit newbies, there are credit-builder loans, which act sort of like a combination of forced saving and reverse borrowing. Here, you make timely monthly payments on the loan until it's paid off, and then you get the money. Look for credit-builder loans with the lowest interest rates and fees, often available at small banks and credit unions. Another option: Get a cosigner—another person who guarantees that the loan will be paid back in full—for a regular loan.

In some cases, regular bills you pay (such as rent, utility bills, and cell phone bills) can be used to build your credit. Look into programs like Rental Kharma, RentTrack, and Experian Boost to see if your bills apply.

HOW TO INCREASE
YOUR CREDIT SCORE

No matter how high or low your credit score is, there are steps you can take to increase it. This won't happen overnight (and don't believe anyone who says it can), but it can happen pretty quickly. You may be able to increase your score by 100 points or more in just a month or two.

Once you do, you may be surprised by how much it helps your finances. A better credit score could save you money on car insurance or help you avoid paying a utility deposit next time you move. Best of all, it will help you get lower interest rates every time you borrow—and that will save you tons of money in the long run.

Review Your Credit Report Every Year
Your score gives a quick snapshot of your credit reputation, backed by a full credit report that contains a detailed collection of personal and financial information. With all of the credit-based

information flying around, it's not really surprising that most people's credit reports contain mistakes (such as charges that aren't yours or a bill that's paid but listed as open). Those mistakes can lower your credit score, so it's in your best interest to find errors and get them off of the report as quickly as you can. Your credit report can also alert you to fraud and identity theft, and it should be one of the first things you look at if you suspect foul financial play.

You're entitled to one free credit report every year from each of the three major credit-reporting bureaus. The easiest way to get them is to order a free comprehensive report online at www.annualcreditreport.com. You can also order a report from each of the three bureaus individually through their websites: www.equifax.com, www.experian.com, and www.transunion.com. If you do find mistakes (and you probably will), your best bet is to notify any one of the three bureaus by certified mail. You'll find a good sample letter and instructions on the FTC website at www.consumer.ftc.gov.

Pay on Time and Pay It Down

Increasing your credit score can take some time, but there are two steps you can take to really jump-start the process.

First, get current with all of your bills, and stay current by making *every* payment on time and in full. If you know you're going to be late or short with a payment, be proactive and contact the creditor *before* your account becomes delinquent; creditors will often work with you to protect your credit score if you let them know what's going on.

Second, reduce your credit utilization below 30 percent; it's one of the quickest ways to boost your score. The best way to do this is by paying down debt without taking on any new debt (by using credit cards or applying for new loans, for example).

ASSETS VERSUS EXPENSES

Keep or Consume?

The main difference between assets and expenses is time. Assets have sustained worth; they last a long time. Expenses get used up quickly, consumed right away (or very shortly). When you borrow money to fund asset purchases, you walk away with something of value that will last longer than the loan. When you borrow money to fund expenses, you'll have nothing (of value) to show for it, but you will still have debt. To make borrowing productive (rather than destructive) to your finances, use it to acquire a portfolio of wealth-building assets and avoid using it to cover expenses whenever possible.

BORROWING TO BUY ASSETS

The key to successful borrowing is simple: Borrow money to buy assets that will gain value or produce income. The flip side of that is to not borrow money to purchase assets (physical or intangible items of value that last for at least one year) that will lose value. Of course, there's no crystal ball to tell you whether a specific asset will definitely gain or lose value, but there are some general rules. For example, new cars always lose value while real estate gains value over time; of course, not every house will be worth more than someone paid for it, and some classic cars can gain considerable value over time. The trick lies in knowing when an asset is more likely than not to gain or lose.

Houses, Cars, and Physical Assets

When you borrow money to buy an asset, you pay more for it (the only exception is no-interest loans) than its price. When the asset you've bought comes with wealth-building potential, it may offset the borrowing costs; that's an overall win for your net worth. Here, borrowing as little as possible at the lowest rate and for the shortest time possible offers the biggest benefit to your wealth. Plus, if the asset does end up losing value, the damage will be less.

When you borrow money for an asset that you know will lose value, that chips away at your net worth even more than if you'd paid cash for the asset. The best example of this is cars, which most people borrow to buy. When you need an asset and have to borrow to get it, the financially sensible thing to do is buy the least expensive version of the asset that you can. For example, you may need a car, but you don't *need* a brand-new BMW.

Before you borrow the money, consider the total cost compared to the asset's value and the opportunity cost: Is a $50,000 car worth more to you than a stress-free retirement (for example)? The answer to that is purely personal—just check in with yourself before you borrow money for an asset that can't add to your wealth and could leave you in a less-secure financial position.

Investing in Yourself

Education is an asset. A business you've built is an asset. When you borrow money to invest in yourself and your future, you're debt funding an asset, even though it's not something you can touch. While it makes sense to borrow money for these assets, many people over borrow and end up stuck with debt they can't reasonably manage. Before you borrow for education or to start or expand a business, weigh the borrowing costs against the financial benefits.

Make sure the education you're getting gives you the opportunity to earn more money than you could without that degree. Consider the probability that your future earnings will outpace the money you've borrowed. Create realistic plans and projections to make sure that money you borrow to funnel into your business will be transformed into revenues that will more than cover the loan expenses. For the loan to be a good financial move, the benefits must outweigh the costs.

BORROWING TO PAY FOR EXPENSES

Expenses have no lasting value; they're consumable items that range from food to electricity to pencils. Borrowing money to pay for expenses is one of the fastest paths to financial insecurity. In fact, the number one rule of wealth building is to never spend more money than you earn. When you have to borrow money to cover your regular expenses, you're doing just that: spending more than you earn.

On top of that, loans made to cover expenses are generally unsecured (like personal loans), revolving debts (like home equity lines of credit), or both (like credit cards). These types of loans come with the highest interest rates, even for people with good credit. Over time, the expenses paid with borrowed money may end up costing you two or three times (possibly even more) than if you'd paid cash. That's a bigger dent in your net worth for something with no future value.

If you need to borrow to cover your basic monthly expenses, break out of that cycle as soon as possible. With a combination of spending less money and bringing in more money, you can change your financial position. Then you have the choice to borrow money on your own terms when you want to and not because you need to.

Graduating with Credit Card Debt

College students are increasingly turning to credit cards to cover living expenses, and many are using multiple cards. Only 51 percent plan to pay off their balance in full any given month. And 36 percent of college students rack up more than $1,000 in credit card charges before they graduate (according to a report by EVERFI).

MAKING MONEY ON THE DEAL

Taking the OPM Path to Wealth

When you can earn money using other people's money (OPM), you're on the fastest path to building wealth. It's a tool that billion-dollar corporations and the wealthiest people use to increase their fortunes, and you can use this strategy to your advantage as well. The trick here is to use their money to increase your net worth. That starts with qualifying for the best possible terms, like ultra-low interest rates, and buying assets that will increase in value, supply cash flow, or both.

TIME AND LEVERAGE

To make the most of OPM, you want to use it for as long as possible for free (or nearly free), and earn more on the deal than you're paying. Use OPM along with your own savings to buy things that will increase your net worth. As you build up more wealth, you'll be approached with different types of lucrative opportunities. On your way there, you can take advantage of the types of OPM that are available to you right now.

Zero Percent Borrowing Buys You Time

As long as you have the means and drive to stick to a payment plan, zero percent borrowing offers one of the easiest ways to start increasing your net worth. You'll need stellar credit and steady cash flow to pull this off, along with the willpower to pay off that loan without triggering interest (either by missing a payment or extending beyond the free period). As long as you can do that, zero percent borrowing allows you to use your money to earn money for you (in retirement or investment accounts, for example) while acquiring an asset you can use. Zero percent financing doesn't come around every day, but when it does—and you *know* you can manage it—use it to further your finances.

The Power of Leverage

In the world of finance, leverage means using a little bit of your money and a lot of someone else's to buy wealth-producing assets. For example, if you have $50,000 cash to invest, you could buy $50,000 worth of stock or you could use that money as a down payment on real estate worth $250,000 and borrow money to finance the rest. That second example uses leverage, and it's a key principle of wealth building: using borrowed funds to purchase a larger portfolio of assets than you otherwise could.

RENTAL REAL ESTATE

Investing in rental real estate sets you on one of the most well-worn paths to wealth. The fastest way to move down that path is with borrowed money, which lets you transform a relatively small down payment in to a large, income-producing property.

The true beauty of this strategy is that you've borrowed the money, but your tenants pay back the loan for you. You take on the risks of owning the property and owing the mortgage, but gain a combination of increased wealth and steady income. With rental real estate, you also have the ability to use home equity loans for quick access to cash when you need it. Again, tenants will pay back the loan, making it a double win for your financial position.

You can also pull equity from one property to use as a down payment for another, for increased use of leverage. Before engaging in this potentially risky strategy, run some numbers to make sure that the combined rents will cover all of the loan payments associated with your properties. Between the banks lending the money and the tenants paying back the loans, you've built wealth by almost entirely using other people's money.

Leverage Can Go Bad

When real estate values are on the decline, leverage can switch to the dark side. That's because the borrowed amount may be greater than the current market value of the property, which can lead to losses. A similar effect happens when a rental property sits vacant, and there's no rental income to cover the loan payments.

BUILDING A BUSINESS

Unlimited Income Potential

Starting and building up a business is much easier with a cash infusion, and that often requires a small business loan. Your company will launch faster and further when you have enough cash on hand to cover payroll, inventory, and marketing expenses. That frees up your energy to focus on growing your customer base and implementing sales strategies rather than fretting about income that isn't coming in.

Getting business loans can be tough and sometimes expensive (especially for start-ups, as compared to expansions); after all, most small businesses fail within the first few years. However, with a solid business plan that demonstrates clear profit potential, you can leverage your loan into a thriving business that can fund your family and your future.

CASH AND INCOME

New businesses struggle to come up with cash and create income. Taking out a business loan can help make both of those easier without diluting your ownership stake or putting your personal financial health at risk. A loan brings a much-needed cash infusion to your company, which frees up energy and assets that can be used to generate income—the income that one day will provide all the cash flow your business needs to become self-sustaining and provide you with a steady, sizable paycheck.

Providing Crucial Cash Flow

Running out of cash is a key reason small businesses fold, even if they're otherwise successful. Borrowing money to cover this cash gap can get your business through the lean times so you don't miss out on eventual success. The most important things here are to borrow enough money and to do it before you're out of cash.

Once you have the loan, don't pay it back too quickly. That sounds like the opposite of good advice, but in the earliest stages of your business, cash flow can be more important than profitability to stay afloat. Stretch out payments when your business is generating minimal cash on its own, and ramp up once the company has become self-sustaining.

Debt versus Equity Funding

There are two ways to fund your business: debt and equity. With debt, you borrow money and pay it back with interest, which increases your expenses and decreases your profits. With equity, you sell a piece of your company to someone else. However, many business owners prefer debt funding to maintain total control over their companies.

Creating an Income Stream

The main point of starting a business is to generate an independent income stream, where you're not dependent on the whims of an employer and your earnings aren't limited to what they're willing to pay. To that end, the potential profit improvement should outweigh the costs of the loan, even if that doesn't happen immediately. To get the most bang out of your borrowed bucks, you'll need a focused plan that spells out how the loan proceeds will be used to increase your revenues and profits. When that connection is clear, you'll be able to develop a sustained income stream.

FUTURE WEALTH

Even in the early stages of your business, it's smart to have thought out a beneficial exit strategy. That could mean turning the business over to your kids or other family members or selling it for a (hopefully) hefty premium. Either way, a successful exit takes a lot of preplanning, especially because your business may be the most valuable asset you have. Whether you plan to hand it down or auction it off, your business needs to be able to run without you when you're ready to step aside.

Family Legacy

Wealth takes time to build, and it often takes generations to secure true and lasting wealth. Many families launch small businesses as a way to prosper now and create a productive nest egg for their children and heirs. Though more than 70 percent of family businesses lose traction in the second or third generation, those that continue can supply employment and income well into the future.

While creating a successful company is difficult, sustaining a legacy is even more so, but it can be done with clear communication and proper succession planning. Unfortunately, while 72 percent of small business owners intend to hand off their companies to the next generation, only 57 percent have succession plans in place (according to the National Bureau of Economic Research). You can increase your family's future success by working with experienced financial and legal professionals to develop a legacy plan that works for both you and your children.

One Brick at a Time

One of the most well-known legacy businesses is The Lego Group, which has been owned by the Kristiansen family since it was founded in 1932. The company was launched in Denmark and now has offices in countries all around the world including the US, the UK, and China.

Funding Your Retirement

When you're ready to retire, your established business can fund a financially stress-free retirement. You have two main options, though only one gives you a truly no-worries retirement. You can still own the business (or a stake in it) without working there and collect a portion of the profits, or you can sell.

If you sell the business, you can do that outright (all at once) or through a financing deal (where the new owner pays you over time). If you want to go this route, be prepared to be flexible with your timing. Just like a down market can affect the value of your investment portfolio, a down economy can similarly affect the amount you can get for your company. You'll also want to avoid the need for a fire sale, where you want to get out *now* so you're forced to look at offers you'd otherwise never consider.

Chapter 3

Student Loans

Americans owe more than $1.6 trillion in student loan debt. That's spread out among more than forty-four million people, and for many it poses an enormous financial burden. Student loan debt keeps people from saving for retirement, buying homes, and having children. This current financial crisis has spawned headlines like "Pay Off Your Student Loans in Three Easy Lifetimes" (*The New Yorker*) and "Trevor Noah Explains Why Student Loan Debt 'Is the New Herpes'" (*HuffPost*).

Student loan debt can be overwhelming and challenging, but it doesn't have to decimate your financial future. If you're already feeling clobbered by it, there are things you can do to take control of the situation. And if you haven't yet begun to borrow, you can avoid the crisis completely by taking full advantage of all of your college funding options.

MINIMIZE YOUR COLLEGE COSTS

School on the Cheap

Student loan debt is out of control. For many people, these oversized debt burdens cripple their finances for decades and make it impossible to buy homes or save meaningful money for retirement. High tuition costs are a big part of the problem. The average total cost of education (tuition, fees, meals, and housing) for an in-state student at a public college runs $25,290 (according to ValuePenguin) and $40,940 for out-of-state students. Private colleges cost even more, averaging $50,900 for a four-year degree. One of the best ways to minimize student loan debt is by downsizing college costs from tuition to books to everyday expenses.

SLASH TUITION COSTS

The best way to minimize tuition costs is to apply at the most affordable schools, which normally means state schools in your home state. Even then, the combination of tuition, fees, housing, and everything else can run high enough to make avoiding potentially overwhelming student loans impossible. Unless, that is, you take prudent steps to slash tuition costs even further.

Start with Community College

The most affordable education starts with community college. Fifteen states already offer some form of free (or heavily subsidized) tuition for two-year degrees, and at least twenty more have such plans in the works. Even without a partially free ride, community college tuition and fees run much lower than four-year schools.

Using community college to satisfy all of the general education classes you'll need for your four-year degree (make sure they're transferrable to the school you want to attend) will save you thousands of dollars. You can also get an associate's degree in your chosen field for under $10,000 and skip the bachelor's degree (for now or forever) without sacrificing your earning potential. In fact, according to the Bureau of Labor Statistics, there are at least eleven fields where an associate's degree can score you an annual salary of at least $55,000. Combine that with a lack of student loan debt, and you'll be much further along on the road to financial independence.

Other Ways to Reduce Tuition Costs

Whether or not you go the community college route (which I did, with great results), there are other things you can do to cut tuition costs. Not all of these are available everywhere or apply to everyone, but there are probably at least a few that most people will be able to take advantage of.

- Dual (parallel) enrollment, where students take college courses for credit while still in high school
- Tuition waivers, often available for public service employees (like police officers) and sometimes their children
- Sibling discounts, possibly available to students with a sibling already at the college *if you ask for it*

- Tuition reimbursement, where your employer pays for all or a portion of your college education
- Online courses, which are much less expensive than equivalent courses taken at school and can more easily fit into a work schedule
- Tuition-free programs, available in some states for four-year-degree seekers and may require on-campus employment as an offset

HACK EVERY COLLEGE EXPENSE

Tuition isn't the only huge expense of college; it's just the biggest. Living on campus can add thousands of dollars to your college costs, but sometimes that option makes the most sense. Then add in textbooks and regular living expenses, from food to laundry to transportation, and costs can spiral out of control. Luckily, there's a way to hack virtually every college-related expense if you know where to look.

Housing

On-campus housing has a lot of social benefits but comes with a hefty price tag. If you can reasonably live at home, it's by far the lowest-cost option. Barring that, with on-campus housing, the more roommates you have, the less expensive your room will be. Check to see if your school offers monthly billing for dorm rooms. This little-known option could mean the difference between adding housing into your student debt (and paying interest on it for years) or paying for it as you go.

After your freshman year, consider applying to be a resident assistant (RA), which can score you free (or nearly free) room and board. Off-campus housing may seem like a cheaper option, but that's not always true. Remember to consider things like Wi-Fi, utilities, and transportation to and from campus when comparing costs.

Food

If you get a meal plan, use it; many work on the use-it-or-lose-it principle. Going with a meal plan is convenient for people who will eat most of their meals in the dining hall. When you don't use up your daily (or weekly) points, grab milk, cereal, fruit, and snacks to bring back to your dorm. If you have access to a kitchen, buying groceries and making food will generally be a cheaper option than even the least expensive school plan (especially true for picky eaters).

Books

As for books, go for used texts whenever possible. When no used versions are available, look into book rentals, which can also conserve money and save you the hassle of selling the books when you're done using them. You may also be able to find e-versions of your books, which are less expensive. Save big on used books, ebooks, and rentals on Chegg (www.chegg.com) and Amazon (www.amazon.com).

Search Out Student Discounts

Student discounts are plentiful, so take advantage of them every chance you get. From retailers like Apple and Amazon to airlines to fun stuff like movies and ball games, you can find student discounts for almost anything. You can find a comprehensive list of discounts at www.dealhack.com.

GET MONEY

The flip side of reducing college costs is increasing the funds available to pay for them. Here there are two basic options: Get a job or get financial aid. To qualify for school-related employment and most grants or scholarships, you'll need to have completed your FAFSA (more on that in the next section). As a lot of jobs and aid are granted on a first come, first served basis, it pays to file your FAFSA as early as possible.

Get a Job

Most schools offer part-time work-study programs to students with financial need. This is typically done through the Federal Work-Study Program, but some schools offer additional employment opportunities. Work-study is available to undergrad and graduate students, whether they attend full- or part-time. Jobs are typically on campus but may be off campus with local nonprofits or service agencies. In some cases, jobs may be with private companies if they further the student's education in their chosen major.

If you don't qualify or don't get selected for work-study, look for part-time, weekend, or summer work that won't interfere with your class schedule and study time. Many campuses are surrounded by restaurants and stores. Other common student jobs include babysitting, tutoring, and driving gigs like Uber, Lyft, and food-delivery services.

Apply for Grants and Scholarships

Grants and scholarships are sources of financial aid that, unlike student loans, do not have to be paid back. Both offer money to students based on need; scholarships may also be offered to students based on merit or other qualifications. Apply for as much free financial aid as you can, as soon as you can. Like work-study, many require a completed FAFSA as part of the application process.

Remember, grants and scholarships are not just for freshmen, so keep applying every semester. Good websites to search for aid include www.careeronestop.org, www.fastweb.com, and www.collegescholarships.org.

FILLING OUT THE FAFSA

The Gateway to Student Loans

FAFSA stands for Free Application for Federal Student Aid, and it's the form virtually every college uses to determine how much any student is eligible to receive in total aid. The FAFSA asks for a lot of information, so be prepared to spend some time with it. It can be overwhelming, but the website is fairly easy to use and you don't have to do it all in one sitting. Most important: Fill out the FAFSA as soon as you can, because your aid package depends on it. FAFSA season starts on October 1 for the *next* school year (so your 2020 FAFSA is for the 2021–22 school year, for example).

FAFSA BASICS

Before you get started, you'll need to set up your FSA ID (username and password) on https://fsaid.ed.gov. Once you have that, you can begin entering your personal and financial information into the FAFSA. Because it's set up as a smart form, it may ask additional questions based on information you supply; if some information doesn't apply to your situation, the form will skip those questions. Once it's completed and signed, the information will be sent to all the schools you list.

Gather These Documents

You'll need information from several different sources to complete your FAFSA, and even more if you are considered a dependent student (which most students under age twenty-four are). One parent of each dependent student will need their own FSA ID to report parents' information. Before you log in to work on the form, have these handy:

- Social security number
- Driver's license
- Prior year's federal income tax return (2019 tax return for 2020 FAFSA, for example)
- Prior year's W-2 forms
- Prior year's untaxed income
- Current bank statement
- Current investment account statement

Parents of dependent students will also supply income, tax, and account information on the FAFSA.

You're FAFSA Dependent If...

Students under age twenty-four are considered dependent *unless* they're married, have nonspouse dependents, are veterans or active-duty military, or are orphans. Less than 15 percent of students under twenty-four qualify as independent each year.

Where to Get Help

The first F in FAFSA stands for "free," and there's a lot of free help available if you have trouble filling it out. Your first stop is the Federal Student Aid website (www.studentaid.ed.gov) where you'll find direct links to the FAFSA, a wealth of information on the process for students and parents, and a FAFSA app that walks you through the forms. You'll also find a link for the IRS Data Retrieval Tool, which auto-fills in the tax return data so you don't have to worry about typing a number wrong (which can get your application rejected).

For more assistance, visit the Form Your Future website (www .formyourfuture.org) to find a complete FAFSA guide written in simple, straightforward (nongovernment) language. The site also has a list of online and in-person resources by state, including events designed to walk families through the FAFSA process, normally held at local high schools.

UNDERSTAND YOUR AWARD LETTER

Once you've submitted your completed FAFSA, the schools you've been accepted to will begin to send you financial aid letters (sometimes combined with the acceptance letter). These aid letters will be jam-packed with information, and it's very important to read through them so you can make an informed comparison. While people tend to zero in on the total aid offered, that is not the most important number. Instead, focus on the difference between the total school cost and the aid offered; a higher-cost school could actually end up being the most affordable choice.

Not All Aid Is Equal

Student aid is a broad term that includes grants, scholarships, work-study, and loans. Your aid letter may include a combination of these, and will list the exact amount each will contribute toward your education—but they are not really equal contributors. Grants and scholarships are free money that does not need to be paid back. Some scholarships come with strings (like maintaining a minimum

GPA), and you can lose that money if you don't comply. Work-study offers you limited earnings to help offset college costs, but you will be giving up social and study time to earn it. Student loans, whether they're federal or private, need to be paid back with interest, even if you don't finish school.

Know Your COA and Your Cost

Your aid letter will also include the cost of attendance (COA) and the amount you'll have to pay (your cost). The COA is an estimate of how much you'll pay to go to that school for one year. It normally lists tuition, fees, and room and board but may not include things like books and supplies. Some costs may turn out to be different if your class schedule changes or you end up in a different dorm room, for example. The difference between your COA and your financial aid (if you choose to accept what's offered) is your cost, the additional funds you need to come up with through either savings, additional scholarships, or more private loans.

HOW STUDENT LOANS WORK

The ABCs of Borrowing

For many people, student loans are the first debt they've ever had to deal with, and they're not quite sure how the loans work. With federal loans, the money you borrow gets sent straight to your school's financial aid office. Private loans may send the money to the school or to the borrower, who then has to pay the school. When loan proceeds are paid directly to schools, they apply the funds to tuition, fees, and possibly room and board. If any money is leftover, that goes to the student.

Most undergrad student loans come with ten-year terms, meaning you have ten years once you leave school (plus a six-month grace period in most cases) to pay them back. All student loans come with interest, but how that interest adds up depends on the type of loan you have.

DIFFERENT TYPES OF STUDENT LOANS

There are two main categories of student loans: federal and private. The vast majority of student loans are federal, making up about 92 percent of the total (according to MeasureOne). Federal loans cover around forty-three million borrowers for $1.4 trillion (as of December 2018). Private loans are much less common, making up 7.63 percent of total student debt for a total of $119 billion.

Federal Loans

Federal student loans often come with lower interest rates, better loan terms, and much more payment flexibility. The interest rates on these loans are fixed (they stay the same over the whole life of the loan) and determined by Congress. In most cases, students (even those without any credit history) won't need cosigners or credit checks (except for PLUS loans) to secure federal loans.

With most federal loans, you won't have to start paying them back until after a six-month grace period once you've left school (for any reason). In some cases, interest will begin accruing from the day your loan is disbursed, even if you're not required to begin making payments yet. You'll get a schedule from your lender or loan servicer spelling out when that first payment is due along with how much and how often you'll need to make payments.

Private Loans

Private student loans are just what you'd think: loans offered by private lenders like banks, credit unions, and sometimes schools. The specific lender sets the loan terms, so there's a lot of variation among private loans. Interest rates tend to be higher than those on federal loans (sometimes almost as high as credit card rates). Also, many private loans come with variable interest rates, which means the interest rate and the monthly payment may fluctuate over the life of the loan. Private loans require credit checks and frequently call for cosigners.

Another key difference with private loans is that you may have to start making payments while you're still in school. Other private loans follow the federal model, though, and allow for a six-month payment grace period after you leave school. Read through your loan documents carefully to make sure you understand exactly when and how you need to begin repaying your loans.

THE LOWDOWN ON STUDENT LOANS

Like other kinds of debt, student loans come with some basic common factors: loan balance, interest rate, loan term (how long you have to pay it back), and repayment schedules. From there, student loans (especially federal loans) behave differently than other debt.

Student loans start with your financial award letter, when you decide to accept loans as part of your payment to the school. From there, you sign loan documents that include all the rules governing your loans and your promise to repay them as stated. This is where many students (and some parents) get hung up: They sign without fully understanding how the loans actually work.

When Interest Starts

One of the most important things to know about your student loans is exactly when the lender will start charging interest (also referred to as when interest starts accruing). Most student loans start accruing interest the day the loan gets disbursed, and the borrower is responsible for paying that interest. The main exception comes with federal subsidized loans, where the government picks up the tab for any interest that builds up while you're not expected to be making payments (while you're still in school or during deferment periods).

When Payments Start

You won't have to start making payments on most federal and some private student loans until six months after you leave school. Some federal loans, including parent PLUS loans, may call for payments to start right away. Check with your loan servicer to find out your first payment date to make sure that you don't miss it.

If your loans are unsubsidized, interest starts accumulating right away. That interest gets added to your loan balance, so you owe more by the time payments officially begin. You can make payments to cover that interest (or at least a portion of it) even though you're not required to, and that will help keep your student loan debt from ballooning.

Once you're required to start making payments, do it. If you don't make your payments on time, your loan will be delinquent, and you'll be charged late fees. If you stop making payments, your loan will go into default, and that will have a long-lasting effect on your credit and your finances.

Grandparents with Student Loans

Older adults (age fifty and up) owe $289.5 billion in student loan debt, according to the American Association of Retired Persons (AARP). That's due to a combination of borrowing for others (like children and grandchildren) and extended repayment periods on their own student loan debt.

GOING DEEPER ON FEDERAL LOANS

Borrowing from the Government

Student loans offered by the US Department of Education come in different types under the William D. Ford Federal Direct Loan Program, and it's important to understand what sets them apart from each other. Undergrads are eligible for different loans than graduate students, professional students, or parents. Students with financial need may qualify for subsidized loans. No matter which loan type fits your needs and circumstances, you need to know how it works.

DIRECT SUBSIDIZED AND UNSUBSIDIZED LOANS

Direct Loans are the number one choice of college students, largely because of their low fixed interest rates, the fact that you don't need a credit history or a cosigner to get one, and you have the option of waiting until you're done with school to start paying them back. The catch: The maximum loan amount is limited. The caps run between $5,500 and $12,500 based on your dependency status and class year.

Subsidized Loans

Undergrad students who need financial help to cover their college costs may qualify for Direct Subsidized Loans. With this loan program, the government pays all of the interest on your loans until it's time for you to start making payments.

The maximum amount you can borrow under this program depends on what year of school you're in:

- $3,500 for the first year of undergrad
- $4,500 for the second year
- $5,500 for the third year and beyond

Subsidized loans also come with a total combined cap of $23,000. To learn more about subsidized loan guidelines and requirements, visit www.studentaid.ed.gov.

Unsubsidized Loans

Direct Unsubsidized Loans are available to both undergrad and graduate students, regardless of need, as long as they're enrolled in degree programs and attend school at least half-time. With these loans, the borrower is responsible for all of the interest that accrues on the loan from the moment it's disbursed. If you don't make interest payments while you're in school or during your six-month grace period, the accumulated interest will be added to your loan balance.

DIRECT PLUS LOANS

Sometimes, Direct Subsidized and Unsubsidized Loans just don't cover the whole cost of school—particularly grad school. When that happens, students or their parents can apply for PLUS loans. Like other federal loans, PLUS loans require a currently completed FAFSA. These loans do require credit checks, and people with not-great credit histories may have to take extra steps to qualify. PLUS loans cost more in both interest and fees, and require quicker payments (often sixty days after disbursement); they look more like private loans than federal loans in many respects.

PLUS versus Private

If you've borrowed the maximum in Direct Subsidized and Unsubsidized Loans but still need more money to cover your college costs, you'll have to choose between PLUS loans and private loans. If you have excellent credit and the ability to easily make monthly payments, private loans may be the better option, because you'll almost always get a more competitive (lower) interest rate. However, there are several circumstances where PLUS loans may be more beneficial:

- You think you'll need the more flexible repayment options offered only by federal loans (though not all are available for parent PLUS loans)
- You don't have good enough credit to get a low rate on a private loan
- You expect to qualify for Public Service Loan Forgiveness (find out more about this program at www.studentloans.gov)

Parent PLUS

Parents of dependent undergrads can take out loans to cover the balance of their children's college costs, but parents don't get all of the same protections and options as their children would. Parent PLUS loans come with some standard features, like fixed interest rates, loan fees (charged as a percentage of the loan), and the ability to defer payments until your child leaves school. Interest begins accumulating as soon as the money changes hands, so if you decide to defer payments, that interest will be added to the loan balance.

Generally, the school will direct you to apply for the parent PLUS loan on the StudentLoans.gov website (some schools have different procedures). If you're eligible, you'll have to sign a Direct PLUS Loan master promissory note (MPN). Next, funds will be disbursed directly to the school. If the loan proceeds are greater than the costs, the school will either return the money to you or your student (if you authorize that).

It Stays with You

Parents often ask if they can transfer the payment responsibility for parent PLUS loans to their students. The answer: No. While your child can make the payments, or give you the money to do it, the loan remains in your name and tied to your credit history.

MAKING THE PAYMENTS

Learn the Right Way to Pay

Once you're out of school, it's time to start paying down your student loans. Most—but not all—student loans come with a six-month grace period where you don't have to make payments but interest gets charged. If you don't make any payments during the grace period, that interest will get added to your loan balance, and you'll pay interest on that interest. It's in your best interest to start making payments as soon as you possibly can.

With private loans, you have one choice for repayment, and that's based on the terms you agreed to when you signed for the loan. Federal loans offer a lot more flexibility. You can follow the standard plan, the one you originally signed up for, which is the most favorable for your long-term finances if it works in your budget. If you're having trouble making ends meet and making your student loan payments on time and in full, you may be able to switch to a more flexible plan that offers more budget breathing room.

HOW TO MAKE PAYMENTS

Loan payments start with your loan servicer (or servicers). They'll let you know exactly how to make your payments, including how much you have to pay and when your monthly payment is due. They'll also let you know what you can do if you can't make your scheduled payments, as long as you contact them.

Making the payments is easy; remembering to make the payments or having enough money to cover the payments can be harder.

To keep your loan balance from increasing and your credit score from tanking, do everything you can to stay on top of your student loan payments.

Know Your Servicer

Most student loans are handled by servicers (companies that receive and manage payments) rather than the original lenders; they're sort of like middlemen standing between you and the lender. Your servicer is supposed to help you stay current with your loan, help you switch to a different repayment plan if you can't afford your payments, and offer certification for loan forgiveness programs.

To find your servicer, log on to the National Student Loan Data System (https://nslds.ed.gov) with your FSA ID (the same one you used for the FAFSA) and click on the "financial aid review" button. You'll find an "aid summary" chart with details about your student loans. If you click on individual loans, you'll find the loan servicer.

Making the Payments

There are basically three ways to make your student loan payments:

- By check
- Making online payments
- Autopay

Many servicers offer an interest rate discount (usually 0.25 percent) for borrowers who enroll in autopay. This option also ensures you'll never miss a payment or a due date. Make sure to keep enough money in your account to cover your monthly payment so you won't get hit with overdraft fees.

If you opt for paying by check or paying online (where you are in charge of the payments), make sure you do pay every month on time and in full. You are responsible for these payments even if you don't get a bill, so check in with your servicer if you haven't gotten one.

THE STANDARD REPAYMENT PLAN

The standard plan will cost you the least amount of money overall, but it does come with the biggest monthly payments. The payments will stay the same until the loan is paid off. Standard plans come with a ten-year payback period, which officially begins six months after you leave school. Here, "leaving school" means graduating, withdrawing, or cutting back to less than a half-time schedule.

Figuring Out the Interest

Like other term loans (loans that have to be repaid over a specific amount of time), student loans amortize based on the interest rate and loan term. While your loan is in good standing, the interest accrues daily (there's interest charged every day) but it doesn't compound (you don't pay interest on the interest). For most loans, that interest starts the day the loan gets disbursed, so you'll end up owing more than you borrowed by the time the first payment is due.

You can figure out the interest on your loan with a little math. Divide your interest rate by 365 to figure out the daily rate. Multiply that daily rate by your current loan balance to find your daily interest amount. Then multiply the daily interest amount by the number of days since your last payment (usually thirty days). The number you get there will be the interest portion of your loan payment. The rest of your payment goes toward principal, unless you have any outstanding fees.

Pay As Fast As You Can

Since federal student loans don't have prepayment penalties, you can start making payments as soon as you want and as often as you want. Every month, you'll have the option to pay extra, and that amount will reduce your loan principal balance. If you make additional payments during the month, they'll be treated as normal (principal and interest) payments unless you specifically instruct the lender to apply the whole payment to principal (check with your lender about how to do this properly). The faster you pay down the principal, the less you'll pay in interest, and that means more money to put toward your financial freedom.

SPECIAL REPAYMENT PLANS

For a lot of people, standard student loan payments cripple their budgets, especially when they're fresh out of school. That's why federal loans offer several repayment plans and let you choose whichever one you want. You can also switch plans at any time for free. If you're thinking about one of these, try out the repayment estimator (at www.studentloans.gov) to see what your new payments might look like.

The seven nonstandard repayment plan options include:

- **Graduated repayment plan,** where payments start out small and increase every two years with the goal of having the loan paid off in ten years.

- **Extended repayment plan,** where the loan term can be stretched out for up to twenty-five years to keep payments low for borrowers who owe more than $30,000.
- **Pay As You Earn (PAYE) plan,** where monthly payments are calculated every year to equal 10 percent of your discretionary income (according to US Department of Education guidelines), but never more than they would be under the standard plan.
- **Revised Pay As You Earn (REPAYE) plan,** where monthly payments are calculated every year to equal 10 percent of your discretionary income (and can be more than standard plan payments).
- **Income-based repayment (IBR) plan,** where monthly payments are calculated every year to equal 10 percent of your discretionary income (15 percent if your loans are from before July 2014).
- **Income-contingent repayment (ICR) plan,** where payments equal the lesser of 20 percent of your discretionary income or what your monthly payments would equal calculated over twelve years.
- **Income-sensitive repayment plan,** where your loan term is increased to fifteen years and your monthly payments are recalculated annually based on your income.

What Does "Discretionary Income" Mean?

The Department of Education has its own definition for discretionary income. Here, that means the difference between your annual income and either 100 or 150 percent (depending on your repayment plan) of the poverty guideline for your home state based on the size of your family.

While it sounds like some of these are the same, they have different requirements and some slightly different terms. Many of these plans offer loan forgiveness after twenty years of payments. Keep in mind that with *all* of these alternative payment plans, you'll end up paying more overall than if you'd gone with the standard plan. Not all borrowers will qualify for all of the repayment plans. For more detailed information on all of your repayment options, visit www .studentaid.ed.gov.

CONSOLIDATING AND REFINANCING

Magically Change X Loans Into One

When it's time to start paying back your student loans, you want the process to be as easy and inexpensive as possible. Making four, five, or eight different loan payments every month makes it much easier for one (or more) to slip through the cracks, resulting in late or skipped payments. If interest rates have changed since you took out your loans, you may be paying more in interest than you have to.

You don't have to stay stuck with the same loans you started with. There are two ways to transform your loans: consolidation and refinancing. With consolidation, all of your separate federal student loans get rolled into one with one interest rate and one monthly payment. When you refinance, you trade your existing loan (or loans) for a completely new loan with new loan terms. Before you decide to consolidate or refinance, do a little homework to figure out which is the better choice for your current and future financial situation.

CONSOLIDATING FEDERAL LOANS

The primary goal of loan consolidation is simplification, converting multiple loans with different payments and due dates into a single loan that's much easier to handle. Normally, consolidating loans results in a longer loan term, which may help your current finances but at the expense of your long-term financial picture.

To consolidate your student loans:

- You have to be done with school
- Your loans have to be in good standing (not in default)
- You must be making regular loan payments or be in a grace period
- They have to be in your name (for example, you can't combine your loans with a parent PLUS loan)

Federal Direct Consolidation Loan

If you have a bunch of federal loans that you want to blend into one, go with a direct consolidation loan. You won't pay any fees to combine your loans through the federal system, and your overall interest rate won't change, because the new rate is based on the weighted average of your old rates.

Consolidating can lower your monthly payments by extending your loan term for up to thirty years. That may make it easier to fit the loan into your current budget, but will cost you more in interest over the life of your loan. At consolidation time, you also have the option of choosing the repayment plan that best fits your budget.

If you decide to consolidate your federal student loans, you can fill out the direct loan consolidation application online at www .studentloans.gov in about thirty minutes. Avoid using any other service to "help you" consolidate because they will charge you fees.

Consolidation Math

Before you decide to consolidate your student loans, run the numbers through a student loan consolidation calculator to see if it makes good financial sense. You can find good calculators at *NerdWallet* (www.nerdwallet.com) and Student Loan Hero (https://studentloanhero.com).

Keep Some Loans Out of the Mix

Be aware that you don't have to consolidate *all* of your loans, and there are some loans you should leave out. For example, if you have one or two loans with much higher interest rates than the others, you might want to leave those out so they don't skew your new interest rate too high. Also, if some of your loans are on track for forgiveness (such as under the Public Service Loan Forgiveness program), consolidating them will erase all of the credit you've earned. You can learn more about deciding which loans to consolidate from *Money Under 30* at www.moneyunder30.com.

REFINANCING YOUR STUDENT DEBT

The main goal of refinancing student loan debt is saving money. You refinance your loan (or loans) into a single loan with a lower interest rate. This has the double benefit of saving you money in interest over the long haul and reducing your overall monthly payment. Refinancing is an especially good option if your credit score has improved substantially since you took out the loans and you'll qualify for a lower interest rate.

The Only Option for Mixing Federal and Private Loans

If you have both federal and private student loans, you can't roll them all into a federal consolidation loan. This calls for a private refinance, and making that decision can change more than you think. Switching to a private loan strips you of the benefits that come with federal loans, like the option of income-based repayment plans and loan deferment. If you're not 100 percent confident in your ability to cover your student loan payments every month no matter what happens, you may want to keep those federal features for a safety net. Then, it might make sense to consolidate your federal loans and refinance your private loans separately.

For people with good credit, refinancing often works out better financially than consolidating federal loans. Along with a top credit score, you'll need to have a history of making on-time payments and a debt-to-income (DTI) ratio (a measure of how much you owe compared to your income) of less than 50 percent. If you're confident you can do without the protections federal loans offer, you may be able to save thousands of dollars by refinancing. Student Loan Hero (https://studentloanhero.com) offers a calculator with a side-by-side consolidation versus refinancing comparison so you can see at a glance how each option would work.

OPTIONS WHEN YOU JUST CAN'T PAY

There are times when money is so tight that it's impossible to make student loan payments. Don't just stop making payments. Your loan will turn delinquent, then go into default, and that can have lifelong financial consequences that are difficult (but not impossible) to recover from. If your finances have taken a turn for the worse, get ahead of the problem by contacting your loan servicer to see if you're eligible for loan deferment or forbearance.

Both of these allow you to hit pause on your loan payments or reduce your payments to a manageable amount. These options are available for federal student loans, but with private loans it depends on the specific lender and the loan contract. Keep in mind that your loan balance will increase during the pause period due to interest accumulation (unless you have specific types of loans and choose deferment).

Note: The following is based on federal student loans, as terms with private lenders may vary. For more information, visit www.studentaid.ed.gov.

You're Not Alone

According to the Department of Education:

- 3.7 million borrowers have loans in deferment
- 2.6 million borrowers have loans in forbearance
- 5.1 million borrowers are in default

That's 11.4 million borrowers, 26.5 percent of all people with federal direct student loans.

Deferment

If you're struggling to make payments on your subsidized student loans, deferment is the better choice. During deferment, interest will not accrue on subsidized loans, so your loan balance won't grow. There are different ways to qualify for deferment and each calls for a separate request form. Circumstances that qualify for deferment include:

- Attending school at least half-time
- Being unemployed
- Being on active military duty
- Experiencing economic hardship
- Serving in the Peace Corps

Student loan payments may be deferred for up to three years in most cases, sometimes longer, depending on the qualifying event.

Forbearance

If you don't qualify for deferment (and sometimes even if you do), you can get forbearance for your student loans. Forbearance will suspend or dramatically lower your student loan payments temporarily. Unlike deferment, interest will always accumulate and add to your balance with forbearance.

Contact your loan servicer to request forbearance. You may have to fill out a general forbearance application or they may grant it over the phone (it's at their discretion whether or not to grant it, but they usually do). There's no time limit on the forbearance, but try to keep it as short as you possibly can. While this is a better option than defaulting on your loan, it's still a costly choice. The longer you remain in forbearance, the bigger your debt will grow. If you can, use the reduced payment option rather than the total pause for your forbearance to prevent your financial situation from getting even worse.

Chapter 4

Credit Cards

Most people are exposed to credit cards before they have any idea how they work or how to use them properly. We see our parents and other adults swiping a plastic rectangle and getting stuff. For the uninitiated, it looks like they're somehow getting something for nothing, because we never see the money change hands.

That magical thinking can carry into adulthood. When you pay by credit card, it doesn't *feel* like you're spending money. In fact, you're not really spending money—you're *borrowing* money. You know that you'll have to pay the bill eventually, but the promise of small minimum payments can make purchases seem like bargains. Credit card companies are well aware of this psychological disconnect, and they take full advantage of it. That's how so many people end up with overwhelming credit card debt. But if you know how they work before you start using them, you can turn them into tools that help you build up a credit history and improve your financial situation, rather than the other way around.

HOW CREDIT CARDS WORK

The Perils of Plastic

Our wallets are full of small plastic rectangles that seem harmless but can inflict serious financial damage. It's easy to forget you're spending money when you pull out a credit card or (even worse) pay with a phone app (tied to a credit card) or use one-click checkout (tied to a credit card). Every time you swipe that card (or app or one-click), you're borrowing money, and the credit card issuer will let you keep borrowing until you hit your credit limit (and sometimes they'll let you keep going). That convenience comes at a cost, and most people don't realize just how much these loans (yes, they're loans) cost until they're saddled with credit card debt.

CONVENIENCE AT A PRICE

Credit card companies increase convenience at every turn. Their goal: getting you to use your credit card for everything and make the smallest possible monthly payments. They encourage you to overspend by dangling rewards in front of you. They discourage you from paying your balance in full by offering the option of minimum payments, which seem like monthly payments but aren't. Credit card companies like it when you pay late (as long as you do pay), so they can increase your APR and charge you penalties. After all, the more money you owe and the longer you owe it, the more money they make. And they're in this to make as much money off of you as possible.

Easier Than Cash

There are many reasons people use credit cards, but the number one reason is simplicity; it's easier to use a credit card than virtually any other payment method. Credit cards are easier to physically carry than cash, don't limit your purchase to the amount in your wallet, and give you the option of paying now or later (you can make credit card payments every time you use them, if you want to). In some circumstances, paying with a credit card may be your only option. Common examples include booking a hotel room, renting a car, prepaying for E-ZPass, or buying plane tickets (though you might be able to make these purchases with a debit card). Plus, credit cards add a layer of safety. If you lose cash, it's just gone, but if you lose a credit card, you can cancel it and request a new one.

The Cashless Revolution

Though some cities and states have outlawed the practice, many stores and restaurants across the US have gone cashless, which means your money (actual money) is no good there. Those retailers prefer safer, quicker card payments to cash, despite the added expenses attached to receiving credit card payments.

Required Disclosures

Under the Truth in Lending Act, credit card companies must clearly disclose certain information on both their applications and cardholder agreements. Most people skip over this. It's a lot of information and numbers that may not seem important, but they play an enormous part in your financial future. At the very least before you apply for and use the card, make sure you know this information:

- Regular APR (for purchases), which may include multiple rates or a range of rates, and whether that APR is fixed or variable
- Promotional APR, when that promotional rate ends, and what can invalidate the promotional rate (a late payment, for example)
- Penalty APR, what causes it to go into effect (usually missed payments), and how long it lasts
- Grace period, how long you have to pay your full balance without incurring interest charges
- Finance charges, including how they're calculated and the minimum finance charge
- Fees, which must include every fee you could possibly be charged with

This information can protect you from costly mistakes, help you avoid fees and penalties, and help you keep your credit card interest as low as possible.

THE MINIMUM PAYMENT CON

Minimum payments on credit cards are specifically calculated to keep you in debt for as long as possible. It's how credit card companies maximize their profits, by charging you interest for years. If you carry a balance (which is what they want and encourage you to do), everything you buy could end up costing you double or triple (sometimes even more, depending on the interest rate) the original charge. When you stick with their minimum payment plan, you lose money and they win effortless profits.

Minimum Payment Math

Minimum payments are based in part on how much you owe, usually the larger of an extremely small percentage of your balance due or a fixed dollar amount (often $25). You can find the details for your card in your cardholder's agreement in the "payments" section.

Some issuers go with a flat percentage (usually 2 percent, sometimes as high as 5 percent, but that's rare) of the balance due; for example, if you owe $5,000, your minimum payment would be $100 ($5,000 × 0.02). Others go with a lower percentage plus interest, normally 1 percent plus whatever the current month's interest charges work out to. If you're behind on payments, your current minimum payment will also include prior months' missed minimums plus penalties and fees.

Remember, the credit card company's minimum payment amount is for their benefit, not yours. Paying this amount by the due date will let you avoid late payment fees and higher penalty interest rates, but that's all. It will keep you in debt for years (maybe decades) and cost you a ton of money in interest—exactly what the card issuer wants.

The True Cost of Minimum Payments

Credit card statements now come with minimum payment "warnings" that show you explicitly how much making only these payments will cost you over time. Don't just glide over that part of your bill (and, yes, you absolutely must look at your credit card bill every month). The sticker shock might help jolt you into making bigger-than-minimum monthly payments.

If you follow the credit card company's plan and pay just 2 percent of your balance every month, it will take you years to pay it off. Your minimum payment probably just covers more than the prior month's interest charge, making only a teeny dent in the original principal balance. By paying any amount more than the minimum—even just $5 or $10—you'll pay off your credit card debt faster and pay less interest over time.

Consider this example: Let's say you have a $5,000 balance due on an 18 percent credit card, and you don't make any new purchases. If you make their 2 percent minimum payment every month (which starts at $100), it will take you 39 years to pay it off. Plus, you'll pay $13,396.53 in interest, which *quadruples* the cost of whatever you bought. But if you add just $10 a month to your minimum payment, you'll pay off that debt in just six years, and pay $3,460.53 in interest. And if you add $25 a month to the minimum, your debt will be done in just over five years, with total interest charges of $2,693.11. Go online and play around with some credit card calculators to see what an enormous difference paying *any amount* more than the minimum will make. You can find credit card minimum payment calculators at www.bankrate.com and www.creditcards.com.

DIFFERENT TYPES OF CARDS

Pick a Card, Any Card

Credit cards may all look the same, but they come in several different types. Each works in a slightly different way to make them stand out from the pack. Before you settle on a credit card, do some research to figure out which kind of card will work best for your situation. You can choose among cards that help build credit, offer airline miles or cash back, or come with discounts from dedicated retailers. Whichever card you go with, make sure it fits with your spending style and financial plan.

REWARDS CREDIT CARDS

Rewards credit cards give you something in exchange for using your card. The more often you pull out the plastic, the more rewards you can earn. These cards typically offer cash back, points that you can use to make purchases, or a combination of the two. With cash back, you can get your cash directly (like through PayPal or in a check), as a statement credit (using your cash back to pay your bill), or on gift cards. Points are most often associated with airline miles, but they can be used for a wide variety of items depending on the program parameters. The best rewards card for you is the one with a combination of rewards you'll actually use and the lowest annual fees (if any).

Common Rewards Cards
The three most common types of rewards cards include:

- Travel rewards cards that let you earn miles or points toward hotels, airfare, and other travel-related purchases
- Gas rewards cards that offer cash back when you use them to pay at the pump, making them good choices for people who drive a lot
- Cash back rewards cards that give you cash back on a wide variety of eligible purchases, and sometimes offer extra rewards on bonus categories

The Catch

Rewards cards are great for people who pay off their cards in full every month. If you don't, the rewards aren't worth nearly as much as the interest you build up by carrying a balance. It's *never* to your benefit to load up on rewards if you're either overspending or cannot pay your balance in full. On top of interest, some rewards cards charge annual fees. To use those cards to your advantage, your rewards should significantly outweigh the fee you're paying.

OTHER TYPES OF CREDIT CARDS

Rewards cards rank as the most popular cards, but there are a few other kinds of cards as well. Some of these may also wrap rewards into their programs as a bonus for cardholders. The type of card that will work best for you depends on your budget, spending style, and current credit situation.

Charge Cards

Charge cards don't technically fall into the credit cards category, but they're close enough. With charge cards, you have to pay your balance in full, every month. There's no interest because you cannot carry a balance on a charge card. The point of a charge card for the borrower is the float: You still have the ability to buy now, pay later; it's just that the pay later comes sooner than it would with a credit card. You need stellar credit to qualify for most charge cards.

Charge cards come with a lot of benefits. They're more convenient than carrying cash. They give you a paper trail for every purchase, and are easy to track for budgeting purposes. They normally offer lots of perks and bonuses to cardholders, as they want to encourage spending. They come with either no limit or a very high spending limit. On the flip side, charge cards almost always come with (often steep) annual fees; they have to make their money somehow.

Secured Credit Cards

If you have no credit or bad credit, using a secured credit card can help you build a solid credit history and better financial habits. These are essentially prepaid credit cards: You give the card issuer a cash deposit as collateral before you can use the card. Since the issuer is covered whether or not you make on-time regular payments, these cards are much easier to qualify for than regular credit cards. If you're using the secured card to build or repair credit, it's crucial to make every monthly payment on time and in full.

Retail Cards

Some credit cards are issued by retailers (or e-tailers) rather than banks or credit card companies. With these retail cards, you have an account directly with the store (or other type of retailer) and can only use the card at that store. Many retail cards offer rewards points and dedicated coupons to encourage cardholders' loyalty and boost spending.

Not Really a Retail Card

Retail cards are not the same as branded general credit cards. For example, a Target REDcard is not the same as a Target Mastercard; the REDcard can only be used at Target, while the Mastercard can be used anywhere those cards are accepted.

THE COSTS OF CREDIT CARDS

Interest, Fees, and Penalties

Borrowed money comes at a cost, and credit cards are no different. What sets them apart is the way they charge interest and the myriad (and sometimes hidden) fees they charge that can quickly increase your balance due. When you know how much using your credit card will truly cost, you can make better decisions about when and how to use them. Once you see how the interest and fees work, you can figure out how to minimize those costs, maybe even get them down to zero (yes, it's possible to use credit cards for free). You can control how much your credit cards cost you.

HOW CREDIT CARD INTEREST REALLY WORKS

Credit card interest doesn't work the way most people expect it to. If you have a credit card with a 16 percent APR (annual percentage rate), you probably think you'll be charged 16 percent interest each year. That assumption makes sense, but it's wrong. Credit card companies use that APR to come up with a *daily* percentage rate (you can figure it out by dividing your APR by 365). They apply that daily percentage rate to your average daily balance, another thing that credit cards do differently than other loans.

The average daily balance is what it sounds like. The credit card company figures out your balance every day, starting with the prior month's balance due and adding activity day by day for the full billing period. Purchases increase the daily balance, and payments lower it. At the end of the billing period, they add up all of the daily balances and divide the sum by the number of days in the billing period. That little equation gives them your average daily balance. The final step in calculating your monthly interest charge involves multiplying your average daily balance by the daily percentage rate and then multiplying that result by the number of days in the billing period.

It's convoluted and complicated, and they use this method on purpose to charge you more interest. Plus, since payments are due toward the end of the billing period, they steer you toward keeping your daily balance high for most of the month.

Credit Card Interest Compounds

When you run a balance on your credit cards, you're paying interest on the interest they charge you; that's called compound interest. Depending on how frequently the credit card company compounds interest (which should be spelled out in your cardholder agreement), you could even be paying interest on interest that was charged only days ago. That can bump up your total interest charges even higher than your APR. The only way to avoid it is to pay off your full balance every month.

Watch Out for Teaser Rates

Credit companies may lure you in by offering teaser (promotional) rates—interest rates that are much lower than the normal rate—for a fixed period of at least six months. Teaser rates are designed to encourage overspending. Many cards offer zero percent teaser rates, which lull people into thinking they won't pay any interest on the purchases they make. But as soon as that teaser period expires, the full rate kicks in, often causing interest shock. If the balance charged during the teaser rate period hasn't been paid off by then, the new higher interest rate takes over, adding substantially to the cost of your purchases.

CREDIT CARD FEES

Credit cards come with a broad range of fees, and not every card charges the same fees. Fees break down into two main categories: usage fees and penalty fees. Usage fees are charged based on actions you take with your credit card. Penalty fees are linked to late and missed payments.

You can easily avoid usage fees by avoiding these more expensive actions unless they're absolutely necessary. When you do need to use them, remember to account for the fee so you aren't surprised by it when your bill comes. There's also an easy way to avoid penalty fees: Make at least the minimum payment on time every month.

Usage Fees

There are two types of usage fees associated with credit cards: annual fees and transaction fees. These will all be disclosed in your cardholder's agreement, so make sure to familiarize yourself with that information before you start using the card. Knowing when you'll be charged a fee can help you avoid them.

Some credit cards come with annual fees, ranging from about $30 to more than $500. These are automatically charged to your card once a year, and they're usually connected with charge cards and rewards cards. If those rewards exceed the annual fee, even a high fee may be worthwhile. Some cards will waive the fee for the first year, giving you that much time to use the card for free (and then you can cancel it).

Other common usage fees include:

- Cash advance fees, usually 3–8 percent *plus* a dedicated (usually higher) interest rate
- Balance transfer fees, usually 3–5 percent
- Foreign transaction fees, usually 1–3 percent

Foreign Transaction Fees

You may be charged foreign transaction fees if you use your credit card outside the US or if you buy something using foreign currency (like ordering something from a Canadian website and paying in Canadian dollars, even if you're sitting in Baltimore when you do it). These fees cover the cost of currency conversion rates and usually run between 1 and 3 percent.

Penalty Fees

Credit card companies charge a whole host of penalty fees, and these can be much higher than their usage fees. You'll pay extra for everything from late payments to going over your limit to returned payments (like bouncing a check). These fees can be pretty steep too. For example, the company can charge you $28 the first time you miss a payment due date, and $39 any time after that. On top of that, making a late payment can set you up for a penalty interest as well, and those average around 30 percent.

Sometimes, credit card companies will waive these fees the first time they're charged, but you have to reach out to them and ask them to do it. Even more important, ask them to waive the penalty interest rate (if that applies). You can also choose to have charges rejected if they'll put you over your limit.

USE YOUR CREDIT CARD EFFECTIVELY

Make the Card Work for You

Though the odds seem stacked in the credit card company's favor, you can turn that around and use your cards to your advantage. When they're used the right way, credit cards can help strengthen your credit history and boost your score. They can give you some interest-free float time, the period between when you buy something and pay for it, improving your cash flow situation. Plus, when you earn rewards, you'll actually be profiting by using your card properly.

BUILDING CREDIT

Most people's first venture into the world of borrowing money involves a credit card. That makes credit cards their first chance to start building credit, so it's crucial to understand what factors into a credit score (in order of importance):

- Payment history
- Utilization (how much of your credit is being used)
- How long you've had credit
- New credit
- Credit mix (different kinds of debt you have)

Payment history and utilization are by far the two biggest contributors to your credit score, so these are the ones you really need to keep an eye on to create a positive credit history.

Never Late, Never Skipped

The number one rule in building credit is to make every payment on time. Even one skipped payment can tank your credit score and stain your credit history for years to come. By only using your credit card to buy things you can afford and always making payments on or before the due date, you'll be well on your way to establishing a favorable credit history and top credit score.

Use whatever tricks you need to in order to make sure you're never late with a credit card payment. Mark it on your calendar, set a reminder in your phone, or set up scheduled payments from your checking account for at least the minimum payment due.

Watch Your Utilization

Credit scores rely heavily on utilization, which means the amount of your available credit that you're using right now. If you have a $3,000 credit limit and your current balance is $1,500, your utilization equals 50 percent. You're best off keeping your utilization under 30 percent, both for your credit score and your overall financial health; lower is even better. You can track your utilization by knowing how much credit you have available on all of your cards combined and what their combined outstanding balance due totals.

If you see your utilization creeping up above 30 percent, start taking steps to lower it. The first step is to stop using credit cards, and the second step is to work on paying down your balances.

IMPROVING YOUR FINANCIAL SITUATION

When you make a point to only use your credit cards for things you could afford to pay for with cash and pay the cards off in full every month, you open up a new passive income stream. It won't be enough to retire on, but it will provide tax-free monthly income (at least it's not taxable *yet*). Using your cards strategically also helps you better manage your cash flow, the timing of when money flows in and out of your accounts. This combination of smoother cash flow and an income bump can make using your credit cards a financial help rather than a financial drain.

Use the Float

Almost all credit card issuers offer a grace period, usually around thirty days of interest-free time between when you make charges and pay them. By spending mindfully and using your cards for only the things you would be buying anyway (like groceries and electricity), you won't overspend and blow your budget. As long as you pay your balance in full before the grace period ends, you won't pay any interest to the credit card company. This time gap can help you manage cash flow by adding more flexibility to your budget, but it only works to your advantage if you use your cards wisely.

In most cases, you can choose your credit card payment date. Pick a date that comes a day or two after your paycheck hits your checking account so you'll be sure to have the funds needed to cover your credit card bill.

Earn Rewards

When used correctly, credit card rewards programs pay you money to use your credit card. You can earn cash and points toward purchases by simply using your card. The trick is to do this strategically, so it doesn't end up *costing* you money.

Step one involves knowing which kind of rewards you'll actually use; if you rarely travel, for example, earning airline miles won't be useful. Step two involves your spending habits; you want a rewards card that fits the way you already spend money. The third step is to choose a rewards card that doesn't charge an annual fee (unless the rewards will greatly outweigh the fee). When you choose rewards cards that will really work for you, you can use them to pay your regular bills and make your regular purchases, so you earn money every time you buy something.

Finding the Best Rewards Card for You

With hundreds of rewards card to choose from, it can be tough to pick the right one. You can find some great advice and prescreened picks online at trusted websites like *NerdWallet* (www.nerdwallet.com) and *Money Under 30* (www .moneyunder30.com).

Remember, rewards programs only work to your advantage when you only use the credit card for things you'd be buying anyway and you pay your balance in full every month.

USE ALL THE CARD BENEFITS

Credit cards offer more benefits than most people realize, far beyond rewards points. When you pay off your full balance every month, you can take advantage of all of these extra services for free.

Common credit card benefits include:

- Travel insurance
- Baggage delay insurance
- Travel accident insurance
- Rental car coverage
- Price protection
- Theft protection
- Extended warranties
- Fraud liability protection

These extra benefits often get overlooked, but they can be very valuable for cardholders. Look through your cardholder agreement to see which of these benefits and protections come with your credit card.

BALANCE TRANSFERS

The Credit Card Shuffle

If you have credit card debt—meaning you carry a balance on your card(s) rather than paying it off every month—you might benefit from a balance transfer. This lets you "refinance" high-rate credit card debt for a *temporary* zero percent (or other extremely low) rate. That gives you the opportunity to pay down your debt much faster, because you won't be throwing as much of your money at interest rather than principal.

Sounds straightforward, but like all things credit card–related, balance transfers come with multiple catches. Deals that seem great may not be. Confusing terms can trap you with even more debt. Before you transfer your balances, make sure to read all of the fine print and compare different transfer options. That way, you'll get the biggest benefit out of your balance transfer.

HOW BALANCE TRANSFERS WORK

You've probably gotten balance transfer offers in the mail or in your email, offering a zero percent APR if you move over debt from a competing credit card. It sounds like a great deal, trading 16.99 percent debt for zero percent debt, and paying no interest at all for six to eighteen months. These deals can help you reduce crippling credit card debt and finally help you get ahead financially *if you use them wisely*. That's harder to do than it sounds, but when you go into it with foreknowledge and a clear plan, you can use balance transfers to your advantage and make a serious interest-free dent in your debt.

Save Money and Pay Off Debt

Sky-high credit card interest charges can make it extremely hard to pay off your debt. The minimum payments barely cover the current interest, leaving pennies to pay toward principal. You can make slightly more progress by making more than the minimum payments, but still a large portion of every payment will go toward interest. That's where the zero percent (or even a very low rate) balance transfer card comes in so handy, as long as your goal is to fully pay off the debt that you transfer during that promotional period.

Once you transfer high-rate credit card debt on to a no-interest card, every dollar of every payment will go toward your debt. That lets you pay your debt down much faster and at a lower cost. For example, let's say you owe $4,500 on an 18 percent credit card. If you can afford to pay $300 a month, it will take you eighteen months and cost $636 in interest. If instead you transfer that $4,500 balance to a zero percent card with a 3 percent transfer fee, you'd pay off your balance in fifteen months and it would cost you $135 in interest.

Choose the Best Transfer Card

Before you pick a balance transfer card, figure out how much you want to transfer and how long it will *realistically* take you to pay that off. For example, if you can afford to pay $250 a month toward this debt and you want to transfer $3,500, you'll need a transfer card that offers that zero percent rate for at least fourteen months.

Don't discount cards that charge balance transfer fees in exchange for a long-term zero percent rate. These fees usually run between 3 and 5 percent of the amount you transfer; so, for example, you'd pay $60 if you transferred $2,000 with a 3 percent fee. You'll still save money because the transfer cost (almost) always comes out to much less than the interest you would have been charged.

Do look at any other fees associated with the new card. For example, if the transfer card comes with annual fees, remember to factor that into your repayment plan. You'll also want to be aware of any late payment fees, just in case.

DON'T GET CAUGHT IN A TRANSFER TRAP

Balance transfer cards are full of pitfalls that can derail your financial plans. Be aware of these traps, and avoid them at all cost or you may end up deeper in debt than when you started. Though your paydown plan starts with choosing the right balance transfer card, all of them come with these same potential dangers.

Pay Your Bill! Transfers Take Time

Balance transfers don't happen instantly. They can take up to two weeks. If cards you're transferring balances *from* have payment due dates during that time, make those minimum payments. Otherwise, you'll get hit with late payment fees, which can go as high as $39.

Watch Your Payments

Once you've done a balance transfer, do not miss a single payment due date. Being late by even one day will eliminate your zero percent interest rate, the whole point of the transfer. Plus, most cards will also charge you a late payment penalty, which will add to your balance due.

To avoid this trap, schedule automatic monthly payments from your checking account that cover at least the minimum payment due. Set a reminder for yourself so you can make sure you have enough in your checking account to cover that payment.

Know the Time Frame

Before you make the transfer, figure out how much you can devote to each monthly payment in order to be done by the time the zero percent rate disappears. Make sure that you pay off the full transferred balance during the promotional period. The split second that period ends, the rate will go sky high.

Beware, some cards will charge you interest retroactively on the unpaid balance. That means you'll suddenly owe six (or twelve or eighteen) months' worth of interest on the remaining balance due. And like all other credit cards, unless you pay the card off in full, you'll end up paying interest on that interest.

Don't Use the Card for *Anything*

I can't stress enough how important this is: Do not use your balance transfer card for anything at all until after you've paid off the full transferred balance.

First, new charges on this card will be paid before any money goes toward your transferred balance. For example, if you use the balance transfer card to buy $100 of groceries and make a $200 payment toward your debt, the first $100 of your payment goes directly toward that new charge.

Second, if your payment isn't enough to cover 100 percent of the new charges, those charges will start to rack up interest at the regular card rate, not the zero percent promotional rate. That means less and less of your payments will go toward your transferred debt, jeopardizing your entire paydown plan.

GETTING OUT OF CREDIT CARD DEBT

Join the Zero Balance Club

You have credit card debt. It's a financial fact that can feel like failure. Being in debt often triggers feelings of anger, guilt, blame, and shame. You may feel hopeless if your debt seems overwhelming, like you'll *never* be able to get a handle on it. Those negative emotions make it harder to face your debt and may keep you from taking steps to get rid of it.

As hard as it is, try to put emotions and self-blame to the side. What really matters here is what you do next. Every step you take—no matter how small—to address your debt moves you closer to conquering it. Every extra dollar you pay lowers your debt and the future interest on it. And if you're reading this, you've already taken the first step toward fixing the problem.

KNOW YOUR DEBT INSIDE AND OUT

To start your credit card debt demolishing campaign, you'll need a complete listing of what you owe. Sounds simple, but facing this debt can be very hard when it's all laid out in front of you. (Some people I work with take this step with a drink or cupcake—it helps take the edge off.)

The next step is even harder. After you get a handle on how much you owe, it's important to figure out how and why you accumulated more credit card debt than your budget could handle. Facing your credit card debt this way can help prevent the same thing from happening again. The best way to do that is to stop using credit cards; go cold turkey, and cut them up if you have to.

List It

Before you can make your debt list, you need to gather your most recent credit card statements. If you don't get paper versions, you'll find them online on the card issuers' websites.

To list your debts, make a grid with five columns. It can be on paper, in a spreadsheet, or in an app. For each debt, include the name, balance due, interest rate, minimum payment, and payment due date. Total up all of the minimum payments to get a sense of the least amount you'll put toward debt every month.

Now you have a complete picture of your credit card debt, a crucial step toward defeating it. The numbers may shock you when you see it all together like that, and you may feel discouraged. Take the next step anyway. You can do this.

Look at It

Now that you know the numbers, it's time to take a look at how and why you got here. Credit card debt can build for a number of reasons, and the two main causes are uncontrolled spending habits and emergency situations.

Both credit card companies and retailers do everything in their power to keep you swiping. They don't just encourage spending, they specifically encourage credit card use and mobile payments because those don't really feel like you're spending money. That leads to overspending if you aren't careful and don't stick to a budget. Start *really* paying attention to how much money you spend—you'll be surprised.

Another major feeder of credit card debt: emotional shopping (a.k.a retail therapy). Brain science tells us that shopping can increase feel-good brain chemicals like dopamine, and when you're feeling down, that instant shot of happiness makes you feel better in the moment. The trick is to be aware of that and find mood-boosting alternatives that don't increase your debt load. That's not to say that *all* emotional shopping is bad; only when you spend more than you can afford on something you don't even really want.

Weird as it sounds, scientific studies show that people spend more (and not just on food) when they're drunk or hungry. Don't shop when you're hungry, and never bring credit cards with you when you'll be drinking.

Emergency credit card spending sounds unavoidable, but that's not entirely true. Building up a hefty emergency fund can help you weather emergencies without going into credit card debt. That doesn't mean you can't ever use credit cards to cover emergencies; it means you can avoid getting trapped in credit card debt because of an emergency. Even if you use your credit card on the spot, your emergency savings lets you pay it off rather than running a debt-building, interest-heavy balance. Once your credit card balances are cleared, start building your emergency fund right away.

Apps Can Help

You can use apps to help organize your debt and keep track of it. Look at Debt Free, Debt Payoff Pro, and Debt Manager, and choose whichever feels most comfortable to you. These useful apps each cost $0.99 and let you work with an unlimited number of debts.

MAKE A PAYDOWN PLAN

When you're ready to start paying down your debt, make a plan that you can stick to. The best plans involve focusing on one debt at a time (your "focus" debt). When you zero in on a single debt, it's easier to make and see progress. Plus, it's much less stressful to face a molehill than a mountain.

The two most popular paydown plans are the snowball method and the avalanche method. Either will help you dig your way out of debt, so choose whichever feels more comfortable for you. Avalanche normally works a little bit faster and saves you a little more interest. But it's usually easier for people to stick with the snowball method because there are more victories early on.

Both methods work well, and you don't have to lock yourself in; you can switch between them whenever you want. The trick for success here is to pick the one you think will be easier to start with, and then get started.

No Matter Which Plan You Choose

Whichever method you go for, make sure to do these four things:

1. Pick one focus debt that you'll put extra money toward
2. Throw every dollar you can at that focus debt
3. Make multiple payments throughout the month (rather than one on the due date) to minimize the next month's interest charge
4. Make on-time minimum payments every month on every debt

That last point is important. Any skipped or late payments will be hit with expensive penalties that take your debt in the wrong direction and make it even harder to pay down. Avoid even the possibility of late payments by setting up automatic payments to cover the minimum for every credit card, including the focus debt.

There is a fifth thing to do, but this one can be extra tough: Stop using your credit cards except for actual emergencies. It's practically impossible to pay credit card debt off if you're adding new charges every month.

The Avalanche Method

With the avalanche method, you'll rank your credit card debts by interest rate, from highest to lowest, and focus on the most expensive debt first. Regardless of how big that debt is, you'll save money in interest, which leaves more money for paying down the balance.

You can find your current credit card interest rates (sometimes listed as APR) right on the statements. Pick the card with the highest rate, and start paying that one down as fast as you can. Once it's paid off, you'll move to the next highest rate, and keep going until all of the cards are paid off.

The Snowball Method

If you like extra encouragement and motivation, the snowball method may work well for you. Using this plan, you'll pay down your first focus debt more quickly, and get a sense of accomplishment as you cross it off the list. You'll be able to clearly see your progress, and that little rush (it's true; it's science) will help keep the paydown practice going.

With this method, you'll list your debt in order of balance, from lowest to highest. Your smallest debt will be your first focus debt. Once that one's settled, you'll use the money you'd been putting toward it to pay the next debt on your list (your payments will "snowball"). You'll keep paying off debts and moving down the list until all of the debts are paid off.

Snowflakes

Whichever paydown plan you use, you can sprinkle it with snowflakes any time. Snowflakes are found money you can use to make extra payments on your focus debt. They include things like birthday checks from Grandma, tax refunds, and yard sale proceeds, and can help you pay your debt down even faster.

Chapter 5
Mortgages

Buying a house is probably the most expensive purchase you'll ever make, and usually the lion's share of that purchase will be made with debt. Before you agree to take on that huge debt, make sure that you really can afford it both now and for the next few decades. There are many types of mortgages and dozens of loan features to sort through. Before you start shopping around, figure out which type of mortgage is best for your financial situation and a comfortable (not a maximum) payment your budget can cover.

RIGHT-SIZE YOUR MORTGAGE

Get a Goldilocks Loan (Just Right)

When it comes to taking on a mortgage, you need solid information in your corner. Lenders will offer you the largest possible loan based on how your finances look on paper. Their goal is to lend you a lot of money for a long time and collect tens of thousands of dollars in interest.

Your goal is the opposite: to take out the smallest mortgage you can, and never more than you can easily afford to pay back. That might mean buying a smaller house or looking in an area with a lower cost of living, which might feel disappointing right now but will be a huge stress saver down the line.

WHAT LENDERS LOOK AT

Every mortgage lender uses slightly different criteria when determining how much money and what loan terms they'll offer, but they all look at the same basic information. That starts with your gross income: your total paycheck before taxes, retirement plan contributions, and other deductions are taken out. From there, they try to figure out the biggest mortgage payment you can afford by factoring in things like property taxes, your current debts, and your credit score.

The Front-End Ratio

Lenders first look at how much of your annual gross income can go toward repaying the loan to determine your maximum mortgage payment. They base that on the full mortgage payment, known as PITI, which includes:

- **P**rincipal
- **I**nterest
- Property **T**axes
- **I**nsurance (both homeowner's and mortgage insurance)

They compare your gross income to the PITI to come up with the front-end ratio, the percentage of your income needed to cover the mortgage payment. Many lenders allow that ratio to range between 30 and 40 percent—but that's much higher than most borrowers can easily afford.

For example, let's say your gross annual income (which may include your salary, bonuses, business income, side gigs, alimony, and child support) comes to $75,000. That works out to $6,250 per month. Thirty percent of that comes to $1,875, and 40 percent comes to $2,500 per month. Remember, though, that's based on your *gross* income, not how much money you actually take home, so their idea of affordable may not mesh with your budget.

The Debt-to-Income Ratio

Your debt-to-income ratio, or DTI ratio, measures the percentage of your gross income that goes toward paying debt. Most financial experts and lenders recommend keeping your DTI ratio under 36 percent of your gross income, but some lenders will let your DTI ratio be as high as 43 percent. You can calculate your DTI ratio by dividing your total monthly debt payments by your gross income.

What counts as debt here?

- The new mortgage payment
- Loan payments (including car, student, and personal loans)
- Credit card payments
- Alimony and child support
- Any other monthly obligations (like back tax payments)

Total up your monthly debt payments, then divide that number by your monthly gross income. For example, if your total debt payments come to $2,600 and your monthly gross income is $6,250, your DTI ratio would be 41.6 percent.

Credit Score

Your credit score plays a huge role in determining how much the mortgage will cost you. Lenders look at this to assess your risk factor—how likely you are to pay the mortgage in full and on time every month. Your risk factor translates directly into your interest rate: People with lower credit scores almost always pay higher interest rates. That can add thousands, even tens of thousands, of dollars to the total lifelong cost of your mortgage.

Most conventional lenders look for credit scores of 620 or above. Government-sponsored loans (like Federal Housing Administration [FHA] loans) allow for lower credit scores, lending to people with scores in the 500s.

RUN YOUR OWN NUMBERS

When you're considering taking out a mortgage, you'll need to do some different math than the lenders do. Your number one question will be how much mortgage your family can truly afford, not how much mortgage can you get. Your calculations will be based on your net income, the amount of money you have left after taxes and other deductions, because that's the only money available to put in savings or pay bills. You will look at all of your expenses, consider all of your financial plans and goals, and come up with a more realistic maximum mortgage payment for your budget.

Remember, lenders may seem to care about what's best for your budget, but they really care about selling you a loan so they can make money. It doesn't seem like that when you're trying to get approval; it feels like you're trying to convince them to finance your house. Remember this: The bank is not on your side, and the bank always wins.

Buyer's Remorse

According to the NerdWallet 2019 Home Buyer Report, 34 percent of first-time home buyers don't feel financially secure after purchasing a house. That remorse doesn't only hit first-timers, though. The study also reports 25 percent of American homeowners feel that way after their home purchase.

What DTI Leaves Out

Not only does DTI consider your gross income, it also leaves out most of your regular monthly expenses. It doesn't take into account your cell phone bill, cable and Internet, groceries, utilities, prescriptions, school clothes, vet bills, or the dozens of other things you spend money on regularly.

First, consider the difference between your gross and net income. For most people, that difference runs between 25 and 30 percent after federal and state income taxes, Federal Insurance Contributions Act (FICA) taxes, and deductions for retirement plan contributions and health insurance are subtracted. That means that right off the top, you already have 25 to 30 percent less money available to cover expenses.

Next, think about any new expenses you'll have. For example, if you're moving to an area with a higher cost of living, factor that into your budget. If you're moving from a rental, add in the costs of maintaining and repairing the place you plan to buy, which may include:

- Yard work
- Snow removal
- Homeowners association fees
- Plumbing and electrical repairs

If you're moving to a bigger place, you'll also need to account for things like higher energy costs and possibly additional home furnishings.

All of these extra costs will flow into your monthly budget and need to be considered when you're figuring out how much mortgage you can afford.

Don't Forget Closing Costs

Closing costs often get overlooked when people are looking into mortgages, but they should be part of your search for the best loan. There are a lot of expenses (like transfer taxes and recording fees) associated with buying a home, and those costs have to be paid at the closing (when all of the legal documents are signed and the big money changes hands). Closing costs normally add between 3 and 5 percent of the sales price to your deal, and if you (as the buyer) are paying the realtor's fees, they can run as high as 10 percent.

Some lenders will offer to "wrap" the closing costs into your loan. That seems like a welcome convenience, but it will cost you a lot more money in the long run in extra interest. A better choice: Find out the total estimated closing costs and bring enough cash to the closing to cover them.

Look at Your Life

Your spending style will also play a key role in the affordability of your mortgage. If you like having a lot of disposable income to spend on going out or buying whatever you want, a large mortgage payment combined with the many other expenses of homeownership can put a serious crimp in that. While you might technically be able to afford the mortgage, it may be all that you can afford if it eats up too much of your income.

Another important consideration: your life stage and goals. Buying a house with a mortgage that tightens your budget could make it much harder to meet other financial or personal goals. If you need your full income or two incomes to cover the mortgage, that could affect your timing for things like having children, leaving a job you don't like, starting a business, or retiring. Think about how the mortgage will fit into—and possibly change—your life plans before you sign on the dotted line.

SAVE UP FOR A SUBSTANTIAL DOWN PAYMENT

Go Big to Go Home

When you're buying a house, part of the money will come from you and the rest will come from the bank. The part that you'll come up with is called the down payment, and the bigger it is, the less you'll have to borrow. You may be tempted to look for a mortgage lender that allows for a very small down payment, but that choice can take a serious toll on your future financial health. The more you scrape up to put down, the lower your payments and your total interest paid will be.

BIGGER IS BETTER

Saving up a substantial down payment sends a clear signal to lenders (and to yourself) that you're ready to buy a home. You've successfully budgeted your money, you know how to manage your income and expenses, and you're actively building your net worth. That dedication scores you some big benefits too. You'll find it easier to get a mortgage, giving you more power to decide which loan you choose to take and a strong bargaining position to negotiate better terms. It may also be easier to get the home you want; sellers (and realtors) tend to prefer buyers who bring more cash to the table. Plus, you'll gain some serious advantages that can affect your financial security for decades.

Lower Rate, Smaller Payments

The most obvious benefit of a higher down payment is a lower loan balance. The less money you borrow, the better it is for your net worth and financial future. With a smaller balance, a bigger portion of every payment you make will go toward paying down principal—and that means you're paying less interest.

That's not the only way you'll save money. A bigger down payment also helps you qualify for a lower interest rate, which can save you tens of thousands of dollars over the life of your loan. Plus, the combination of a smaller loan balance and a lower interest rate translates to a smaller monthly payment, leaving more money in the budget to enjoy your new home.

Lower LTV

Loan-to-value (LTV) ratio is a measure that compares your mortgage balance to the market value of your home (at the time of the sale, market value normally equals the selling price). The LTV ratio will change over time as the market value of your home changes and as you pay down your mortgage. A larger down payment means a lower LTV ratio, and here lower is always better.

The flip side of a lower LTV ratio is more equity (the portion you own free and clear) in your home. Having more equity helps protect you financially by acting as a safety net if home prices should decrease drastically (like they did in 2008). The lower your LTV ratio, the more likely you'll be able to walk away from a depressed home sale with cash, rather than owing the bank more than you sold your house for.

Go for the Full 20 Percent

There's a reason most lenders consider 20 percent to be the magic number: If you can manage to save up that much money to buy your house, you're much more likely to be able to manage the monthly payments without a struggle. That 20 percent also works in your favor, and it will greatly benefit your financial situation both now and in the future.

The Upside Down

When home prices drop, homeowners can end up upside down on their mortgage, meaning they owe more money on their mortgages than their homes are worth. Technically, that's known as having negative equity, and it happened to many homeowners during the 2008 housing crisis.

One of the most noticeable benefits: Borrowers who put down at least 20 percent of their home price don't have to pay private mortgage insurance (PMI). This insurance protects the *lender* if you stop making loan payments, to limit their losses. PMI premiums cost around 1 percent of your mortgage balance every year. The ongoing cost is normally added into the monthly mortgage payment. For example, if you borrowed $250,000 and had a 1 percent PMI premium, your mortgage payment would increase by $208 per month ([$250,000 × 1 percent] / 12).

Playing Devil's Advocate

In some circumstances, you may want to think about going with a smaller down payment.

- To avoid zeroing out all of your savings, which leaves you with no cushion if an emergency occurs (and they always do)
- To buy a home sooner, because saving a "big enough" down payment could take many years

- To buy points, which effectively means prepaying some interest in exchange for a lower interest rate on the mortgage

Even if one or more of these apply, it still makes financial sense to make the biggest down payment you can.

WHERE TO STASH YOUR DOWN PAYMENT CASH

When you're saving up for a down payment, you want that money to be safe, accessible, and growing on its own.

Because down payments usually run to tens of thousands of dollars and can take a long time to save up, you may consider investing those funds in the hopes that they'll grow faster so you can reach your goal sooner. If you don't plan to buy a house for at least ten years, that might be a good place to stash *some* of your down payment. Remember, though, that invested funds can just as easily lose value as gain it—and if you aren't prepared to lose even a dime, this is not the place to house your down payment money.

For most people, the best bet is to use a high-yield savings account, backed by the Federal Deposit Insurance Corporation (FDIC) (for banks) or the National Credit Union Administration (NCUA) (for credit unions), so your money is guaranteed secure. High-yield accounts (as the name spells out) offer much higher interest rates than standard savings accounts—sometimes ten or twenty times higher. You'll find the highest rates with online banks, and it pays to shop around; with so much money in play, a difference of 0.25 percent can translate to hundreds of dollars.

FIXED VERSUS ARM

In Your Best Interest

Traditionally, thirty-year fixed-rate mortgages have been the go-to loans for homebuyers. Now, driven mostly by millennials, adjustable-rate mortgages (ARMs) are gaining popularity. The difference between the two loan types is the way interest is charged, and that can have an enormous effect on how much your mortgage will cost in the long run.

Both types of loans come with advantages and drawbacks, but ARMs also come with an extra word of caution: Make sure you fully understand and prepare for rate and payment changes so they don't blow your budget.

FIXED-RATE MORTGAGES

The vast majority of mortgages in America come with fixed interest rates, meaning that the interest rate on day one is the rate you'll be charged over the entire life of the loan. Fixed interest rates also mean fixed mortgage payments (for the loan itself, not including insurance or property taxes). The biggest benefit of these loans is their predictability, which makes them much easier to budget for over the long haul. For most people and most circumstances, fixed-rate mortgages are the financially safer choice, especially during a low-interest rate environment where rates are more likely to increase over time.

Lock In Your Rate

With a fixed-rate mortgage, the interest rate is locked in for the entire life of the loan. It's in your best interest to qualify for the lowest possible fixed rate. To score the best rate, you'll need

- A 20 percent (or more) down payment
- A FICO score of at least 760
- A solid, steady earnings record (two years of salary or five years of self-employment income)

You can also get a reduced rate by getting a fifteen- or twenty-year mortgage instead of the traditional thirty-year loan. You may also consider paying "points" (sort of like prepaying some interest) to get a lower rate on the loan.

Once you've scored a great rate, you need to lock that in. Closing on a house can take weeks, sometimes months, and rates can change during that period. Rate locks guarantee a specific interest rate on the loan for a set period of time; your rate won't go up *or down* no matter what happens with prevailing rates. Most lenders offer free rate locks for up to sixty days.

Monthly Payments May Change

Most people with fixed-rate loans are unpleasantly surprised when they get a payment change notice from the mortgage company. This happens when your homeowner's insurance and property taxes are paid through your mortgage company. Those costs almost always rise every year, and that leads to a bigger monthly mortgage payment. It does not affect the portion of your payment that goes to principal and interest, only the escrow part of the payment. Be prepared for this annual increase by accounting for it in your budget.

ADJUSTABLE-RATE MORTGAGES

It's spelled out right in the name: An adjustable-rate mortgage (ARM) comes with an interest rate that changes over time. Normally, ARM loans start with an introductory fixed-rate period, and the rate starts to adjust after the fixed period is up. Those introductory rates are often much lower than fixed rates to entice homebuyers, allowing people with less secure finances (such as limited savings or student loan debt) buy houses more easily.

Before you take out an ARM, make sure you understand all of the terms of the loan. ARM loan terms can be much more complicated than fixed-rate loans and include a lot of lingo and numbers that can be confusing. The most important thing to realize: Your mortgage rate will almost always increase (despite salespeople telling you that your rate *might* decrease), and those increases can make the loan much more expensive than the fixed-rate mortgage. You can learn more about ARMs in the free *Consumer Handbook on Adjustable Rate Mortgages* available on the Consumer Financial Protection Bureau website at www.consumerfinance.gov.

Rate Changes

Once the fixed period of an ARM expires, the interest rate begins to change periodically, usually once a year. The timetable is normally right in the name of the loan; for example, a 3/1 ARM has a three-year fixed-rate period followed by a rate adjustment every (one) year, while a 5/6 ARM has a five-year fixed-rate period followed by a rate adjustment every six months.

New interest rates are calculated using a specific formula based on a widely known benchmark market index plus a margin (the fixed percentage that gets added to the index rate). For example, if the index rate is 4.25 percent and the margin is 1 percent, the new interest rate on the ARM would be 5.25 percent; that's called the fully indexed rate.

Rate changes may also be subject to a variety of caps that limit how much the rate can increase. There are three main rate caps available, though not all loans include all three:

- **Initial:** limits the rate increase (or decrease) the first time the loan adjusts
- **Periodic:** limits the increase (or decrease) during a specific period (like one year)
- **Lifetime:** sets a maximum for the interest rate that it cannot exceed

Here's an example of how this all works. Suppose an ARM had:

- An introductory interest rate of 3.25 percent
- A margin of 2.75 percent
- A periodic cap of 2 percent
- A lifetime cap of 10 percent

At the first adjustment, the index rate was 5 percent, so the fully indexed rate would come to 7.75 percent (5 percent + 2.75 percent). The periodic rate cap would limit that adjustment to 5.25 percent (3.25 percent + 2 percent), making that the new rate. Even if the index rate doesn't change again, your mortgage rate would continue to increase until it reached the fully indexed rate.

Payment Changes
When the interest rate on an ARM changes, the monthly payment will change too. When the rate increases, the payment will increase

along with it. If your budget isn't ready for the new payment, that can cause significant financial distress. You can avoid that by keeping track of adjustment dates and carefully planning ahead for payment increases. Make sure you can realistically expect to afford those higher payments—up to the maximum payment—before you agree to the loan.

Many ARMs include payment caps, which limit the amount the monthly payment can change by in an adjustment period. Payment caps are often expressed in dollars rather than percentages, so you can tell how much your payment could increase.

Watch Out for Negative Amortization

Sometimes, the combination of rate caps and payment caps causes a nasty situation called negative amortization. This occurs when the rate increase on your loan would cause a payment increase greater than the payment cap allows. That means your monthly payment won't cover the full interest portion of the payment. The "missing" interest instead gets added to your loan balance every month until the payment adjustment catches up to the rate adjustment. Until the payment catches up, though, you will be making monthly mortgage payments and your mortgage balance will *increase* every month—that's negative amortization.

ARM Indexes

The most commonly used indexes for ARM rate changes include the London Interbank Offered Rate (LIBOR), the prime rate, and the yield on one-year Treasury bills. Those index rates change frequently to reflect current economic and market conditions.

THIRTY YEAR VERSUS FIFTEEN YEAR

How Long Can You Go?

Homeowners tend to flock to thirty-year mortgages. After all, that is the standard, with 90 percent of borrowers choosing the thirty-year option (according to the Federal Home Loan Mortgage Company, commonly known as Freddie Mac). Many potential borrowers may not even realize that there are other choices for mortgage loan terms, and that going shorter can save them tens of thousands of dollars (or more!) over the lives of their loans.

WHICH IS BETTER?

Time affects the total cost of your loan in a few different ways. A longer loan term offers smaller monthly payments. A shorter loan term offers lower interest rates, lower total lifetime interest paid, and faster equity buildup. On paper, a shorter loan term may seem like the obvious winner, but it will limit your financial flexibility and the opportunity to build a more liquid nest egg. The term that's better for you is the one that fits into your overall financial plans and your monthly budget.

A Thirty-Year Loan

Thirty-year mortgages are the gold standard in the lending world, mainly because of the more affordable monthly payments than loans with shorter terms. That's not the only difference, but it is the most noticeable one. Lower payments mean there's more money in your budget available to go toward savings (retirement, emergency funds, college)—but that's only a benefit if you funnel the difference (or at least part of it) into savings. Smaller payments may also allow you to buy a bigger house or take out a bigger mortgage than you could with a shorter loan term.

On the downside, your mortgage will come with a higher interest rate and you will pay substantially more interest over the life of the loan. That money goes straight to the bank, instead of funding your future.

A Fifteen-Year Loan

Shaving fifteen years off your loan term can make a huge difference over the life of your loan. If you can afford those steep monthly payments, it will be better for your overall financial health to go with the shorter loan. For one thing, banks love shorter loans (they're lower risk) and reward these borrowers with lower interest rates, sometimes as much as a full percentage point lower than their thirty-year counterparts. That combined with the much shorter time period means huge savings on interest costs.

Another big benefit: You'll build equity at a much faster pace, as a larger portion of your payment will go toward principal every month. More equity means you're much less likely to end up underwater if housing prices drop and you need to sell. You'll also be in a better financial position if you ever want to take out a home equity loan.

The big (very big) drawback with fifteen-year mortgages is the oversized monthly payment. The average payment on these loans runs anywhere from 35 to 50 percent larger than it would with a thirty-year mortgage, putting these loans out of reach for people on tight budgets. The bigger payment can also make it harder to save for retirement, though the lifetime interest savings and earlier pay-off date can help offset that. If you do go with a fifteen-year mortgage, make sure to have a very large emergency fund (a full year's worth of expenses) available to cover your payments if necessary.

Look at the Difference

Seeing the numbers and how they compare can help you figure out which loan term will work for you. To start simple, we'll look at a $200,000 loan and keep the rate the same at 4 percent for both terms. Using that information:

For the thirty-year loan, the monthly principal and interest payment will be $955, and you'll pay lifetime interest costs of $143,739.

For the fifteen-year loan, the monthly principal and interest payment will be $1,479, and you'll pay lifetime interest costs of $66,288.

By going with the shorter loan term, you'll have to come up with an extra $524 every month to cover the mortgage payment. On the other hand, you'll save $77,451 in total interest costs. Realistically, though, the payment would likely be a little smaller and the total interest savings even bigger because fifteen-year loans have lower interest rates than thirty-year loans.

Too High DTI

If you decide to go for a fifteen-year loan, pay close attention to your DTI (debt-to-income) ratio. Even with a solid gold credit score and a large down payment, the bigger monthly payment on a fifteen-year loan can push your DTI ratio past the lender's cutoff, which can disqualify your application.

MEET IN THE MIDDLE

If the supersized monthly payment of a fifteen-year loan makes you queasy, but you don't want to be on the hook for thirty years' worth of interest, consider a compromise. There are two main ways you can have your mortgage and pay it off too: Choose your own payment or apply for a twenty-year loan. Either way, you won't be saddled with budget-busting mortgage payments, and you'll save tens of thousands of dollars in lifetime interest costs (compared to a full thirty-year loan).

T-Minus Thirty and Counting

Just because you took out a thirty-year mortgage doesn't mean you have to make payments for thirty years. You can enjoy the comfort of a smaller mandatory mortgage payment but make bigger or additional payments if you want to pay your loan off earlier. Every extra dollar you pay reduces the next month's interest charge, which means more of every following payment will go toward paying down principal, and you'll pay less interest over the life of your loan. Since you're making these extra or bigger payments voluntarily, you can skip that whenever life throws you a curveball, and pony up just the regular monthly payment.

Check for Prepayment Penalties

Prepayment penalties (fees for paying down your mortgage early) are strictly limited under current law, but they still crop up on some fixed-rate loans for the first three years. Before you make extra principal payments, check your loan. If the lender does charge prepayment fees, that will be disclosed on every billing statement or in your coupon book.

The Twenty-Year Compromise

Most people aren't aware that twenty-year mortgages exist. In fact, these little-known gems make up less than 1 percent of total mortgage loans. They combine the best parts of the more popular thirty- and fifteen-year mortgages:

- More manageable monthly payments than fifteen-year loans
- Better interest rates than thirty-year loans (but not quite as low as fifteen-year rates)
- Significantly lower lifetime interest costs than thirty-year loans (just a little higher than with fifteen-year terms)
- Fast equity building

Though they're not heavily advertised, most commercial lenders do offer twenty-year mortgages. You just have to ask for the information.

FIND THE BEST LENDER

Shop Around

Mortgage lenders often make prospective homebuyers feel like they're auditioning, like borrowers have to sell themselves to lenders to get approval. That's backward. You're the customer here, and you deserve the best possible mortgage product for your situation. Before you connect with any lender, get prepared. Know what you want, and know what's out there. Come to the table with a sizable down payment and a solid credit score. Then let the lenders sell themselves to you.

DO YOUR HOMEWORK FIRST

At least a month (longer is even better) before you're ready to start shopping for a house and a mortgage, start gathering up intel on lenders and loans. After all, you'll be making a thirty-year (maybe fifteen or twenty) commitment, and that calls for some up-front research. You'll want to compare rates and lender ratings (how easy they are to work with), as well as getting a good sense of the lending arena so you're clear on what you're walking into.

Part of your homework includes strengthening your financial position, the best bargaining chip you can bring to the table. For your financial security, you'll want to keep building up a down payment, a closing cost fund, and emergency savings. For both you and your future lender, you'll want to lower your DTI (debt-to-income) ratio as much as possible and take your credit score as high as it can go.

Crank Up Your Credit Score

Mortgage lenders look at a lot of numbers before they'll agree to loan you money, but your credit score will be front and center. People with lower credit scores will have a harder time getting approved, and they'll also pay a lot more for their loans in the form of higher interest rates. With a score lower than 580, it's nearly impossible to get a mortgage (at least from a reputable lender).

Take this time to work on boosting your credit score so you can qualify for the lowest available interest rates. The best ways to do that include:

- Pay down credit card debt to lower your utilization (the amount of your available credit you're actually using; lower is better)
- Make every debt or bill payment on time and in full
- Check your credit report for errors, and fix them immediately if you find them
- *Do not* apply for any new credit cards or other loans
- *Do not* close existing credit card accounts right now, as that will have the effect of increasing your utilization (by reducing your available credit)

Every step you take to increase your credit score will help you score better loan terms, and that can save you a boatload of interest going forward.

Know the Loan You Want

Lenders will try to sell you the loan that's best for them. Your job is to ignore them and get the loan that's best for you. To do that, you need to figure out the biggest loan and monthly mortgage payment that you know fits comfortably with your budget and your long-term financial goals. Decide whether an ARM or a fixed-rate loan works better for you. Don't let them talk you into going bigger, either on the house or on the loan (and they will try).

LOOK AT LENDERS

It's tempting to go with the first lender who "likes" you, or with the familiar bank that holds your checking account, but that could end up costing you dearly. Rather than focusing on who might approve you, look for the lender that best serves your needs. That could be your credit union, community bank, or an online lender, but you won't know which works best for you until you start comparing. Tap into the wealth of information online to get started; there are dozens of sites that list lenders and rates.

Great Rates, Good Terms

Researching rates online makes a great starting point, but remember that those quotes are estimates and not necessarily accurate rates (and what seems like a tiny difference can cost you thousands of dollars). Once you've gotten a few quotes, you can do a head-to-head comparison of rates, loan costs, and down payment requirements.

You'll also want to look for a lender that's in your time zone (even if they're not local) to make it easier to deal with tight time frames and strict funding deadlines. Keep in mind that some sellers will prefer mortgage lenders they've heard of and are familiar with, which could take you out of the running if you go with a nonlocal lender.

Customer Service Is Key

While your number one focus will be costs, customer service comes in a very close second. You want a lender who will be responsive when you reach out, answer every question you have directly and fully, and not try to push (or sweet-talk) you into a loan that's outside your comfort zone. Ask around, check out Better Business Bureau ratings, and look at online reviews for any lender you're considering. You don't want to get stuck with a lender who misses deadlines or blows off customer questions. This is going to be an important relationship; you don't want to start up with someone who takes days to call you back.

Your Loan Will (Probably) Be Sold

The mortgage lender you start out with may not be the one you end up with. Most mortgage loans are sold to loan servicing companies. When this happens, the only thing that will change for you is where you send the payments; it won't affect any of the loan terms.

Protect Your Privacy

When you're getting online mortgage rate quotes, you're going to have to hand over a lot of information. That usually includes contact information and some general financial information (like the down payment you can afford and your credit score). For you, that's all over with once you're done online, but it's not over for the lenders. Now that they know you're in the market for a loan, they will call and email you—and not just the ones you looked at either. Once you start actively looking for loan information, your information can be sold to other lenders, sometimes a lot of them.

Luckily, there's a very simple way to protect yourself from a deluge of lenders: opt out. The FTC (Federal Trade Commission) gives you this easy out, and all you have to do is ask that no one shares your information. You can do that online at www.optoutprescreen.com or by calling 1-888-5-OPTOUT. Take this step *before* you start collecting quotes.

Mortgage Brokers

If the idea of trying to find the best mortgage hurts your brain, consider working with a mortgage broker to make your life easier. Mortgage brokers act as loan middlemen, connecting borrowers and lenders. Their job is to sort through rates and terms to find the loans that will best suit your needs. They also help you manage all the paperwork, helping you gather documents, pulling your credit score, and running through employment and income verification tasks so you only have to deal with all that one time (instead of every time you connect with a different lender on your own). Mortgage brokers can also keep things on track to avoid delays and snafus for the closing.

On the down side, most mortgage brokers get paid by lenders, which could put their interests at odds with yours; for example, they could steer you toward the lender that pays them the most, even if that's not the deal for you. If you'll be paying the broker yourself, make sure to get a written estimate of the fees up front.

If you decide to go with a broker, shop around the same way you would with lenders. Talk to friends and family for recommendations, look into at least two or three different brokers, and make sure to check their credentials with the state licensing board. After all, this person will have access to a lot of sensitive personal and financial information, so you need to make sure they're legit.

PREAPPROVED AND LOCKED IN

Before you start looking at houses, arm yourself with a mortgage preapproval letter from your lender. Sellers *love* preapproved buyers. That written thumbs-up from the lender shows the seller that you're serious about buying their house, that you've already figured out how much house you can afford and how much money you can realistically borrow. Plus, it benefits you as much by speeding everything up once you're ready to make an offer.

After the seller has accepted your offer and your mortgage has been officially approved, lock in your interest rate. This makes sure that the rate you're expecting is the rate you'll get on your mortgage. The lock-in protects you against rate increases (though it may also trap you if rates decrease), which will bump up your monthly payments as well.

How to Get Preapproved

Getting preapproved for a loan involves virtually the same things as getting final approval. You'll have to supply the lender with a lot of personal and financial information, which will likely include:

- Social Security numbers of all borrowers
- Tax returns for at least the last two years
- Proof of income, which may include W-2s and pay stubs for employees, 1099s and financial statements for self-employed people, or current leases and current market value for rental properties
- Investment account (including retirement accounts) statements for at least two months
- Bank account (checking and savings) information, including two months' worth of statements

- A detailed debt inventory, including creditor information, outstanding balances, and minimum monthly payments
- Divorce records
- Down payment source information, including gift letters (that clearly show the giver does not expect to be paid back)

This process can take anywhere from a week to a few months.

Keep in mind that *prequalified* does not mean the same thing as *preapproved*. *Prequalified* normally just means that you've turned in a complete loan application, which means nothing to sellers. *Preapproved* means the lender has already vetted your application and is prepared to lend you money.

Lock In Your Rate

When your lender locks in your rate, you get a guarantee that your mortgage will come at a specific rate for a certain period of time (usually thirty to sixty days); if you're paying points, that will be part of the rate lock agreement as well. Rate locks protect you from rising interest rates, which may come into play because mortgage loans can take months to close. For example, if you lock in your mortgage at 4 percent for thirty days and rates go up to 4.25 percent during that period, your rate won't change. If rates drop down to 3.85 percent, you're still locked in to the 4 percent rate.

Once you have a signed agreement to buy a property, it almost always makes sense to lock in your rate for as long as the lender will let you, especially if the lender offers a no-fee rate lock. If you're worried about the possibility of rates decreasing, some rate-lock agreements offer "float down" provisions, which relock your loan in at a lower rate, but those options can be quite expensive.

REFINANCING AND PREPAYMENTS

Changing the Terms

You don't have to be stuck with your mortgage for thirty (or fifteen or twenty) years. If your rate seems high or is about to reset higher, you may be able to refinance the loan at a lower rate. If you can easily manage your current mortgage payment but don't want to keep making those payments for decades to come, you can make extra principal payments to get rid of that debt faster. The trick is in figuring out the right move for your overall financial situation, and then taking the steps to make that happen.

DOES IT MAKE SENSE TO REFINANCE?

Sometimes, it makes good financial sense to refinance your mortgage; other times, it doesn't. For this to be worthwhile, the new interest rate has to be low enough to save you money even after taking the new loan closing costs into account. The best way to see if refinancing will actually save you money is to run the numbers using an online refinance calculator. You can find user-friendly tools online at SmartAsset (www.smartasset.com) and Realtor.com (www.realtor.com) that will tell you immediately if a new loan will both lower your payments and save you money overall.

The Right Way to Refinance

If you're going to refinance your mortgage, it pays to do it the right way. On the plus side, refinancing will reduce your interest rate and potentially save you a ton of money in interest. It may also lower your monthly payment, freeing up some room in your budget. But if you don't refinance the right way, it could take a toll on your overall financial picture and your net worth.

Here are some dos and don'ts to help you avoid the potential pitfalls of refinancing.

- **Don't** add more time on to your mortgage, or it will erase the lifetime interest savings. Instead, refinance only for the amount of time you still have left on the original loan rather than restarting that clock.
- **Do** get a written estimate of the closing costs from the lender rather than using your best guess. This helps you save up for the closing costs rather than just rolling them into the loan, which means you'll end up paying decades' worth of interest on them, or sticking them on a high-interest credit card.
- **Don't** take cash out, no matter how tempting that sounds. Remember, lenders want you to borrow more money and they may try to talk you into a cash-out refinance, but that will just increase your debt and the interest you'll pay.
- **Do** shop around for the best loan terms and lowest closing costs, just like you did with the original mortgage.
- **Do** plan to stay in the house for at least two years, or refinancing costs will almost always outweigh the benefits, no matter how low the new rate is.

Sometimes Refinancing Isn't Best

There are some circumstance where refinancing your mortgage is a bad idea, one that could actually bust your budget. The worst case involves prepayment penalties, which take effect if you pay off your mortgage ahead of schedule. These penalties can either be a percentage of your loan balance (usually around 3–4 percent) or a specific number of monthly interest payments (that the lender would be losing). Before you even look into refinancing, find out whether your current loan comes with a prepayment penalty.

In other cases, a refi isn't totally out of the question, it's just a matter of timing. For example, if your credit score isn't *excellent* (750 or greater), you won't be eligible for the best rates. Take some time to boost your score before you apply to refi. Also, take a look at your DTI (debt-to-income) ratio, the portion of your paycheck that goes straight to debt payments. While most lenders will approve you with a DTI ratio of 43 percent, you'll be hit with higher-risk interest rates. Get your DTI ratio down below 36 percent and it's a whole new low-interest ballgame. Finally, if you don't have at least 20 percent equity in your home, wait until you do. Not only will you score a lower rate, you can also say goodbye to your PMI (private mortgage insurance) for a double budget bonus.

The No-New-Loan "Refi"

If you want to pay less for your mortgage but don't want to bother with the hassle of refinancing, ask your lender to lower your rate. For borrowers with perfect payment history (no missed or late payments) and solid credit, lenders will often say yes to this request so you don't refinance with another company.

PAY IT DOWN FASTER

You can pay your mortgage faster by making extra principal payments, called prepayments. Every extra dollar you throw at your mortgage serves three purposes:

- It reduces your debt load
- It increases your equity
- It reduces the interest portion and increases the principal portion of the *next* payment

The earlier you start making prepayments, the more you'll reduce the lifetime cost of your mortgage, which is one of the best things you can do to build your net worth.

How to Make Prepayments

There are a few basic ways to make mortgage prepayments:

1. Apply a big lump sum (like from an inheritance or a bonus) to the mortgage in a one-shot deal
2. Make one (or more) extra mortgage payments every year
3. Add some extra principal on to every mortgage payment you make

Doing this can shave serious time and interest off of your mortgage. For example, making one extra payment every year can knock five years and more than $10,000 off (on average). You can see the impact prepayments would have on your mortgage with an online amortization calculator on sites like *Mortgage Calculator* (www .mortgagecalculator.org) or Bankrate (www.bankrate.com).

Important: Make sure your prepayments go directly to principal. If you make online payments, there may be a box to check that directs money toward principal. If you use payment coupons, there's probably a line for "extra principal." If you're at all unsure, check with your lender before you make the prepayment or they may just apply it toward regular mortgage (meaning principal and interest) payments (like you're paying ahead rather than prepaying).

Watch Out for Prepayment Penalties

Some mortgages come with prepayment penalties, fees the lender will charge if you pay off all or part of your loan early. In most cases, the penalty will only kick in when you're refinancing or paying down a substantial chunk (like 20 percent) of your mortgage ahead of time. Check your loan agreement before you make any prepayment—especially a large one—to make sure you won't get hit with one of these fairly sizable penalties. If you don't want to read through the zillion-page loan document, call your lender and ask.

Chapter 6

Other Types of Debt

Mortgages, student loans, and credit card debt make up the bulk of what people owe, but there are many other kinds of consumer debt, from financing a car to funding a business. Each kind of debt comes with its own twists and different paydown strategies. No matter which kinds of debt you're dealing with, there is a way out. The key is to use the right plan for that debt so you don't end up paying one penny more than you have to.

CAR LOANS

Driving in Debt

Shopping around for a car loan at the same time (or even before) you look for a car can strengthen your bargaining position and lower the total long-term cost of the vehicle. Car salespeople often wrap those two together—the car and the loan—which makes it hard to sort out how much each is really costing you. They talk in terms of monthly payments, trying to keep you focused on that much smaller number. For your financial benefit, you need to look at the full price of the car and the total cost of financing separately.

BEFORE YOU TAKE ON A CAR LOAN

Car loans rank among the highest single debts people take on, with an average of $23,438 (according to LendingTree). When you break that average down further, the results are eye-opening: The average loan to buy a new car runs $32,187, and the average used car loan is $20,137 (as of the first quarter 2019).

Before you borrow more than $20,000 to buy a car, do your homework. Find a car that's suitable for both your life and your budget—don't buy more car than you can afford. Save up as much as you can toward a down payment, and seek out the best loan you can get. It's even better if you can walk into the dealer with a loan preapproval. That neutralizes one of their favorite selling tactics—keeping you focused on the monthly payment instead of the price of the car.

New versus Used

New cars lose a huge portion of their value the second you get behind the wheel, which leads most financial professionals to advise against buying new. In most cases, used cars are much better choices, especially because new cars become used instantly.

New cars do, however, come with two plusses: They have lower repair and maintenance costs, especially for the first few years, and new car loans usually come with lower interest rates. Used cars may come with some question marks (especially if you buy from a person rather than dealer) and higher repair costs. Still, used cars themselves cost much less than new, which can also save you money on total interest even if you're paying a higher interest rate.

Get the Best Deal

Whether you decide to buy new or used, know how much you want to pay before you start shopping. Car dealers like to lump everything together and turn it into a monthly payment, making it harder to see how much you're really paying for the vehicle. It's in your best interest to separate everything out: your trade-in or down payment, the price of the car and any extras, and the financing.

By separating these factors and doing some research, you can figure out a best price for the car you want. Armed with that information, you can start talking with dealers. They may try to steer you toward different cars (the ones they want to sell rather than the one you want to buy) and keep you focused on that "low" monthly payment. Be firm and stick to your plan by staying focused on your budget and the price of the car.

Total Car Costs

The price of the car and the financing are just the beginning when it comes to costs.

Having and using the car also involve a lot of ongoing costs, which include:

- Registration
- Tags
- Insurance
- Gas
- Repairs and maintenance
- Parking

According to AAA, the average cost to own and use a car is $8,849 annually. Depending on the type of car you have, your costs may vary widely from that average. Small sedans, for example, rack up an average $6,777 per year, while midsize SUVs run to $9,697.

Comparing Autos to Autos

It can be hard to compare car prices because even vehicles with the same make and model may come with different "packages" that alter their pricing. You can find good comparison tools online at sites like TrueCar (www.truecar .com) and Kelley Blue Book (www.kbb.com).

NEGOTIATE THE BEST LOAN

The price you pay for your car is half the financial battle. The other half involves the financing. You can plan ahead for this loan by using online calculators (try www.cars.com or www.bankrate.com) to figure out how much loan fits into your budget, both in monthly payments and overall financial plan. Play around with the numbers until you know how much car you can afford and how different rates and loan terms (the number of months until the loan is paid off) will affect both the payments and the lifetime interest paid.

Where to Borrow

Auto dealers seem like the easiest, most convenient place to finance your car, but they don't always offer the best deals (though they'll often try to convince you that they do). You can often get better terms from your bank or credit union or through an online lender. Compare a few different options before settling on a loan. Knowing your choices puts you in a stronger negotiating position and can help you score even better loan terms.

Know Your Terms

You have two key variables to play with in a car loan: interest rate and time. Rates (according to LendingTree) run from 5.33 percent for people with stellar credit to 21.10 percent for people with poor credit (scores under 560); the average interest rate hovers at around 8 percent. Rates will also vary among lenders, so it pays to shop around before you're ready to buy.

Most car loans last between three and seven years. Shorter is better for your net worth, especially because cars lose value quickly (so you could end up owing more than your car is worth). Shorter loans will have higher monthly payments, but save you thousands of dollars in interest over time. If your loan doesn't come with pre-payment penalties, you can pay it down as quickly as you want. Carefully read your loan terms, because prepayment penalties aren't always named that. Also, some lenders will not accept principal-only payments (or won't make it easy to submit them).

When to Refinance

If you're stuck with a high-interest auto loan that has a few years left on it, look into refinancing. The trick here is to lower your interest rate without adding time on to the loan term (which effectively eats into your interest savings). Refinancing your car loan makes sense when:

- Your credit score has improved substantially
- The loan has a very high interest rate (usually a dealer loan)
- Interest rates have dropped and you can get a better rate

In some cases, you may need to refinance your loan because your circumstances have changed and you can no longer afford the payment. Here, it makes sense to stretch out your loan term to lower your payments. Yes, you'll pay more interest over time, but you won't have to miss payments, which will lead to your credit score plummeting and your car being repossessed.

HEL/HELOCS

The Homeowner's "Piggy Bank"

For most homeowners, their home is their biggest source of savings; most of their wealth is locked inside the value of their home. That equity, the portion of your house that you own outright (home price minus mortgage equals equity), can serve as collateral for loans that let you tap into it.

There are two main ways to get cash for your home equity while you still live there: a home equity loan (HEL) and a home equity line of credit (HELOC). People often use the terms interchangeably, but they aren't the same. These two debts come with very different features, but have one very important thing in common: If you don't pay them back on time, you can lose your home.

HOME EQUITY LOANS

HELs are nonrevolving, secured loans. You borrow a specific amount of money one time, using your home equity as collateral. These work just like mortgage loans because they are; in fact, your HEL counts as a second mortgage (the first mortgage is the one you used to buy the property).

While you can use the proceeds from an HEL any way you want, these loans work best when you're using them to make home improvements that will increase your home's value. Otherwise, they'll be more like personal loans that come with losing your house as a consequence of default.

How HELs Work

HELs act like mini-mortgages. You borrow a fixed amount in a single lump sum and pay that back over time with interest. HELs normally come with fixed interest rates, so your monthly payment won't change over time. Your rate will depend on your credit score and on the lender you choose. You can get a good idea of HEL rates online at www.bankrate.com.

HELs can be a good choice when you need to make major home repairs or renovations. If you use the money to "substantially improve" your home, you may be able to deduct some or all of your HEL interest on your income tax return. Qualifying expenditures include things like:

- Putting on a new roof
- Building an addition
- Resurfacing your driveway
- Fully remodeling your kitchen

Keep in mind that the improvements have to be made on the home that's tied to the loan.

Equity Changes

Two key factors come into play when you're calculating your home equity: your mortgage balance and the *value* of your property. Your mortgage balance is easy to figure out; you can find it on your statement or simply ask your lender. Home value is a little trickier. It does not equal the amount you paid for your house. Rather, it's based on the current market value of your home—the amount you could sell it for today. You can get a rough estimate of that by looking at comparable for-sale properties in your neighborhood online (try www.zillow.com or www.realtor.com).

Subtract your mortgage balance (including any other home equity loans you have) from your estimated home value to get your approximate current equity. Lenders may let you borrow a total of up to 85 percent of your home value (depending on your credit history). For example, if your house is currently worth $400,000 and you owe $200,000 on your mortgage, you could borrow up to $140,000 more against your home equity (85 percent of $400,000 = $340,000 – $200,000 = $140,000). The catch: If property values decline, you could end up owing more than you could sell your house for, putting you in a precarious financial position.

If You Sell

If you sell your home while your HEL or HELOC remains outstanding, you'll have to pay it off in full just like you would a regular mortgage. If you owe more than you can sell the house for and you don't have enough cash to pay it off, your lender may agree to convert your loan to an unsecured personal loan at a much higher interest rate.

HOME EQUITY LINES OF CREDIT

HELOCs are revolving loans. They work more like credit cards than mortgages, but your house is still on the line. These flexible lines of credit allow you to borrow money as necessary, up to your limit. You can borrow small amounts over time rather than a big lump sum all at once, giving you both more flexibility and control than you'd have with a regular home equity loan.

HELOCs usually have twenty-five-year terms, split into two distinct parts: the draw period and the repayment period. During the draw period, which usually lasts five to ten years, you can borrow money whenever you want up to your limit. You only have to make interest payments in this period, but you can pay down the balance if you want to; then, you'll be able to reborrow that money. When the draw period ends, you'll switch to the repayment period. Some HELOCs come fully due as soon as the draw periods end, but most amortize the final balance over fifteen or twenty years.

These loans usually come with variable (adjustable) interest rates, though some are fixed and some come with an option to convert to a fixed rate. Those variable rates normally start lower than fixed rates do (similar to adjustable-rate mortgages), then increase as they adjust. You'll only be charged interest on the amount you borrow, not the whole HELOC, and that interest does compound (meaning you can pay interest on interest). Like HELs, if you use these funds to substantially improve the home the loan is tied to, the interest you pay may be tax-deductible.

Don't Overspend During the Draw Period

When you get your HELOC, the lender will give you a line of credit, a total amount available for you to borrow; it works similarly to the limit on your credit card. HELOCs can feel like giant change jars, money that's just sitting there waiting to be spent. If you don't carefully plan and budget how you will use this money, you can easily fall into an overspending trap that leaves you with a large debt that's secured by your home. Don't use your HELOC to cover everyday expenses—this is not the loan to get if you're having trouble making ends meet. If you're unable to make the payments, the lender will foreclose on your house.

Understand Repayment Terms

Many HELOCs also offer interest-only payments during the draw period, which can leave you with an unexpectedly large loan balance when it's done, especially if you've been using the HELOC like a credit card. Once the draw period is up, payments get calculated as they would for any other amortizing loan for most HELOCs. In some cases, though, your HELOC balance could be due in a lump sum as soon as the draw period ends. Make sure you fully understand your repayment terms before you sign the loan documents.

PERSONAL LOANS

For Whatever You Want

Personal loans are unsecured, nonrevolving debts that aren't tied to a specific purchase (like a car or a house). While their interest rates tend to be higher than home or auto loans, they're almost always lower than credit card rates, especially if you have good credit. People looking to consolidate or refinance high-interest rate debt often turn to personal loans, and that can make good sense financially. However, there are times when taking out a personal loan can do more harm than good to your finances, especially if you don't have excellent credit. Before you start a loan application, carefully consider your reason for borrowing this money, whether your budget can manage the monthly payments, and how the extra interest charges will affect your financial situation.

WHEN PERSONAL LOANS MAKE SENSE

Personal loans may make sense when they cost less than the alternative, as long as you can afford to pay them back on schedule. For example, a $5,000 personal loan at 5 percent might make more sense than putting $5,000 on an 18 percent credit card. Along with the interest on the loan, you may also have to pay origination or loan-processing fees; those can range from 2 to 6 percent of the total amount you're borrowing and add to the total cost of the loan.

Refinance High-Interest Debt

Personal loans can make sense when you have high-interest debt, such as credit card debt or payday loans. When the personal loan comes with a lower interest rate than your other debt and you can pay off the balance within a reasonable time period (no longer than five years; three is better), you can save thousands of dollars in interest. However, the money-saving effects of the personal loan disappear if, for example, you continue to use credit cards without paying them off in full every month.

You can also use personal loans to consolidate several high-interest debts into a single loan with a lower interest rate. This makes it easier to track your debt and make sure that you're never late with a payment.

Personal Loans by the Numbers

More than nineteen million Americans owe $138 billion in personal loans (according to LendingTree), one of the smallest slices of the US debt pie. Most of those loans (60 percent) were taken out to either refinance or consolidate other debts.

Bad Reasons to Take Out Personal Loans

Using personal loans as a shortcut to saving up money can take a huge toll on your finances. When you spend the loan proceeds on discretionary purchases and nonessentials, those purchases will end up costing much more money. It may be tempting to borrow money for a dream vacation or a wedding, but you will save thousands of dollars by saving up for big purchases (making monthly payments to yourself before the purchase rather than monthly payments plus interest afterward).

People also commonly use personal loans for paying medical bills, but they're usually not the least expensive option (details on other options come later in this chapter). For example, most doctors' offices and hospitals offer payment plans, often with no or very low interest charges. Dedicated medical credit cards may also be a better option than personal loans, as long as you fully understand their terms and conditions.

"Unsecured" Doesn't Mean No Recourse

Most personal loans are unsecured, but that doesn't mean that the lender can't come after your assets if you don't pay. They can turn your loan over to a collection agency, take you to court, and sue to have your paycheck garnished.

USE CAUTION WITH PERSONAL LOANS

For people with poor credit, the interest rates on personal loans can run higher than credit card rates. When you google rate comparisons online, the rates you'll see are normally the lowest rates the lenders offer—the ones they charge borrowers with good credit. Make sure you know the rate you'll get before you make a decision about the loan. Many personal loans also come with prepayment penalties, which kick in if you try to pay the loan off early. These penalties can be quite high; they're meant to discourage you from paying ahead of schedule, which is normally much better for your financial situation.

Most important, the world of online personal loans is full of scammers and unscrupulous lenders whose aim is to take advantage of people in desperate financial situations.

Steer Clear of No-Check Loans

Instant, no-credit-check personal loans can seem like the answer to a prayer when you're burdened by a huge debt, like a pile of medical bills, and have bad credit. Unfortunately, these easy-access loans can destroy your finances and pull you even deeper into debt. You can find personal loans like these online with a quick Google search, and the results will include dodgy lenders that specifically target people who are desperate for quick cash.

No-credit-check loans can come with enormously high APRs (a mix of interest and fees), sometimes even higher than 400 percent. These are normally short-term loans (no more than three months), but that crazy high APR can make them very difficult to pay back. And even when you pay on time, you could end up paying three or four times as much as you originally borrowed.

Find a Reputable Lender

There are reasonable personal loans available even for people with bad credit (these are not the same as no-credit-check loans). If you decide to take out a personal loan, take the time to find a reputable lender. You won't get instant access to the loan proceeds, but you'll usually have the money within a week.

Your regular bank or credit union should be your first stop, especially if you're a long-time customer. They may be willing to work with you even when your credit isn't good. If you don't have a relationship with a bank already, do some online research to find lenders offering interest rates no higher than 36 percent and reasonable loan fees.

Compare multiple lenders and loans to find the best deal you can get. Websites like *NerdWallet* (www.nerdwallet.com) and *The Balance* (www.thebalance.com) have lender comparison charts and reviews you can use to launch your research. You can also consider looking into peer-to-peer lending at www.lendingclub.com or www.prosper.com. Before you agree to any loan, make sure you understand all of the loan terms, especially the APR and loan repayment period. If you feel confused, pressured, or uncertain, take a step back and do some more research.

PAYDAY LOANS

A Bridge to Difficult Debt

When you're facing an urgent financial crisis, a payday loan may feel like a gift, but it comes with very expensive strings. These loans are quick, convenient, and very easy to get; all you need is a paycheck to qualify. Payday lenders make it seem like you're just getting an advance against your paycheck, but that is not true. Payday loans come with exorbitant interest rates that can make them nearly impossible to pay off, trapping borrowers in a seemingly inescapable loan cycle. If you have any other option, use it instead.

HOW PAYDAY LOANS WORK

The first time most people take out a payday loan, they think it will be the only one they ever get. They borrow a few hundred dollars fully expecting to repay it within a week or two, and then be done. Unfortunately, the finance charges on these loans can make it impossible to pay them back on time and in full, leading to the need for another loan to pay back the first one. Before you even consider a payday loan, understand exactly how they work and the true toll they'll take on your financial health.

The Mechanics

To get a payday loan, you need to show the lender a pay stub and your bank account information. Then, you tell the lender how much you want to borrow, and they put the cash in your bank account immediately. In exchange, you agree to pay the money plus the fee (usually called a finance charge) when you get your next paycheck. Some payday lenders require a postdated check for the total amount due; others ask you to authorize them to remove the money directly from your bank account as soon as it hits. If you can't pay back the loan in full when it's due, the payday lender will usually offer an extension or a "rollover" loan (you get a second loan from them to pay off the first loan).

The Finance Charge

Payday lenders put the loan interest in terms of a fee or finance charge, a flat dollar amount rather than a percentage. For example, the fee may be $15 (or more) for each $100 you borrow. That may not sound like much, but it works out to a pretty horrific annual interest rate. Charging $15 per $100 is the same as a 180 percent annual interest rate, and that's on the low end of the payday loan finance charge scale. Even if you're borrowing that money for just a week or two, you're paying much more interest than you would on virtually any other kind of (nonscam) loan.

ESCAPING THE PAYDAY LOAN TRAP

Because payday loans come with high interest rates in the 150–400 percent range, they can pull you into a dangerous financial trap. Most borrowers are unable to repay the full amount due on their next payday, forcing them into a cycle of repeat borrowing that can last for years; there's no limit on how many payday loans a person can get.

Breaking this cycle can be extremely hard. The only way to get out is to stop getting payday loans. To do that, you'll need enough money to pay off the existing payday loan in full *and* cover your expenses until your next paycheck comes. You'll also need to go on an emergency necessities-only budget and reduce your expenses to the bone during the gap period.

Better ways to get your hands on quick cash include:

- Asking your employer for an advance on your paycheck
- Getting a paycheck advance through apps like Earnin and Dave
- Borrowing from family or friends
- Selling some of your stuff on *eBay*, *craigslist*, or *Decluttr*

Another good option: Look into a payday alternative loan (PAL), available through most credit unions (if you don't already belong to a credit union, join one ASAP). Other banks may have loans similar to PALs, just called something else. Unlike payday loans, PALs are set up to help you pay them off and come with high but reasonable interest rates. They also give you longer (but not much longer) than a single paycheck cycle to pay them back.

Going with any of these options can help you break out of the vicious payday loan cycle. It's extremely hard (and often painful) to escape, but it can be done. Once you're free, and back to a more regular budget cycle, you can start taking steps (like building an emergency fund) to make sure you're never again in a position where a payday loan is your best or only option.

Paycheck Advance Apps

There are several apps that help you access your pay as you earn it, rather than waiting until the end of a pay period. They offer instant cash against your upcoming paycheck and charge low fees. You can learn more about these apps and their (minimal) costs online at websites like *MagnifyMoney* (www .magnifymoney.com) and *Dough Roller* (www.doughroller.net).

MEDICAL DEBT

A Payoff Prescription

More than forty million Americans struggle to pay medical debt, and that includes people with health insurance. Healthcare costs have gone up at an alarming pace. Health insurance covers only part of those costs, leaving patients stuck covering deductibles and co-pays until they reach an out-of-pocket maximum. Unfortunately, many medical issues don't fall neatly within a single plan year, leading to multiple years' worth of deductibles to meet and medical bills to pay. So, it's not surprising (but it is outrageous) that medical bills are the leading cause of bankruptcy.

DEALING WITH MEDICAL BILLS

The medical industry acts like a black box when it comes to billing practices. It's nearly impossible (even for experts) to figure out how much care will cost ahead of time, leaving patients with no idea how to plan for medical costs. And as most medical expenses other than those for routine care crop up unexpectedly, they can't be avoided; if you break your ankle or your kid spikes a super-high fever, it needs to be treated right away, and you deal with the money part later.

Before you pay any medical bill, no matter what size, look at it carefully. Medical billing mistakes are freakishly common (especially if you have a common name). They can lead to you getting billed for procedures you never had or insurance company rejections because of a typo. Paying medical bills you don't need to pay can be double trouble for your budget; just try getting a quick refund from a medical provider or an insurance company for something you paid in error. Any time you get a medical bill, do these four things:

1. Don't ignore it, even if it stresses you out—open it right away and deal with it before it gets sent to collections, messes with your credit, or lands you in court.
2. Make sure the charges match services you got on the dates you got them.
3. Submit it to your insurance company, even if the doctor's office says they submitted it.
4. Check with your insurance company to find out why they aren't covering the bill.

If it turns out that the charges are legit and will not be covered by insurance, either pay the bill or contact the provider to either negotiate a lower charge or set up a payment plan (more on these in a second).

Surprise Medical Bills

Surprise medical bills crop up most frequently due to emergency room visits and hospital stays. These unexpected expenses may be the result of receiving care from out-of-network providers, even if the hospital itself is in your insurance network. As patients rarely have control over who will be treating them in these situations, you could end up with massive medical bills through no fault of your own.

HOW TO PAY OFF MEDICAL DEBT

Medical bills pile up very quickly—even for people with solid insurance coverage. That debt can demolish your budget, wipe out your emergency fund, and max out your credit cards. There are some things you can do to keep that medical debt from thoroughly trashing your finances. The least expensive way involves negotiating with doctors, hospitals, and other service providers; they want to get paid and will almost always work with you as long as you contact them and ask. Other alternatives involve borrowing with interest, either through medical or regular credit cards or personal loans; these options will cost more, but if they can keep you from ending up in court (for a lawsuit or a bankruptcy filing), they may be worth it.

Work Directly with Your Service Providers

Medical service providers have a lot of flexibility when it comes to setting prices, but those prices aren't etched in stone. Those providers can be purposely vague in their billing practices, hoping that patients will just suck it up and pay whatever they charge, but that also gives them a lot of wiggle room in negotiations. If a bill doesn't make sense (like $400 for bandages, for example), call the phone number on the bill (it won't be your doctor) and ask them to reduce the charges. If that's outside your comfort zone, there are companies that will negotiate medical bills for you, but their services aren't free.

When you can't pay a bill all at once, practically all providers offer payment plans. You have to call them to get this set up, and it's best to do it right away before a collections agency gets involved. In most cases, as long as you stay in touch with your providers and make all of the scheduled payments, they won't charge interest or take any other actions to collect the debt.

Borrowing to Pay Medical Bills

If you will need to borrow money to pay medical bills, do it before these outstanding debts start to take a toll on your credit score. You have a few different options here, so do a little research and figure out which will be the least harmful to your finances.

- Use a credit card with a promotional zero percent APR to pay off all the bills, then pay off the credit card before the no-interest period expires (and do not use this card for anything else).
- Apply for a personal loan to cover the outstanding bills if you need more time than a credit card promotional period offers; you'll pay interest, but the payments will be fixed and steady, and you won't have to deal with a sudden spike in the interest rate.
- Pay it through the medical provider's in-house financing, which many providers now offer; these come with higher interest rates than personal loans but often longer payback periods so monthly payments could be smaller.

There are also many government agencies and charitable organizations that offer assistance for paying down medical debt. Find out if you're eligible for Medicaid or CHIP (Children's Health Insurance Program) at www.usa.gov (under the "benefits, grants, and loans" section). Look into similar programs on your state website. You can find a list of charities that help people struggling to pay medical bills on the Cameron's Crusaders website at www.cameronscrusaders.org.

BUSINESS LOANS

Cash for Your Company

It can be tough to get a small business loan from a bank, and it's virtually impossible for companies that aren't yet generating steady sales. When your business needs outside financial support, you have to use every advantage available to score the funding you need for the lowest possible cost. Before you approach any lenders, you'll need to do some serious thinking, planning, and research. That preparation will help you—and your business—succeed.

WHAT TO KNOW BEFORE YOU BORROW

Getting approved for a small business loan requires jumping through a lot of hoops. Entrepreneurs who come prepared have the best chance to secure low-cost loans. You'll need to communicate a clear vision for your company's future and present comprehensive financial statements. And you'll need to provide a lot of documentation that supports your and your company's ability to repay any money you borrow.

Create a Solid Business Plan

Many lenders will request a formal business plan as part of your loan application. If you don't already have a business plan (and you absolutely should), you can find comprehensive guidelines and templates on the Small Business Administration (SBA) website at www.sba.gov.

Know Why You Need the Money

To get a business loan, you have to be crystal clear on how much you need and why you need it. The three most common reasons for business loans include:

1. Starting a business (start-up loans)
2. Covering regular expenses (working capital)
3. Expanding your business (including equipment purchases)

The reason you want the loan will help narrow down the type of loan you can get. For example, traditional lenders rarely offer start-up loans, so you'll need to turn to other sources (like personal loans and nonprofit microlenders).

As for the amount, lenders get uncomfortable when you ask for too much or too little money. If figuring out the sweet spot number proves too difficult, get help from a qualified small business accountant.

Know What It Takes to Get Approved

Small businesses fail more often than they succeed, so lenders (especially banks) demand proof of success (or at least potential success) in order to approve the funding. To qualify for a small business loan at an interest rate that won't drain your budget, you'll need:

- A personal credit score of at least 680 (be aware that applying for business loans can affect your personal credit score)
- To have been in business for at least two years for most bank loans or at least one year for online business loans
- Annual revenues of at least $50,000 (and some lenders have higher minimums of $100,000 or more)

- Enough monthly income and cash flow to cover loan payments plus all regular business expenses

If your business doesn't meet these requirements, you may still be able to get a loan, but expect it to cost more (maybe a lot more).

Know What Documents You'll Need

To get a business loan, you need to demonstrate the ability to pay it back. That means paperwork, and usually a lot of it. Commonly requested documents include:

- Business plan
- Personal and business bank statements
- Personal and business income tax returns
- Personal statement of net worth
- Business financial statements, including a balance sheet, income statement, and statement of cash flows
- Business legal documents, including setup documents (such as articles of incorporation), leases, licenses, customer and supplier contracts, and franchise agreements

Different lenders may ask for more or different documents. Ask potential lenders for a complete list of required documentation so you can have it ready when you apply.

THE RIGHT LENDER
AND THE RIGHT LOAN

Just like with personal borrowing, finding the right loan and lender for your business can make a world of difference. When your business is new or young, you may only be able to secure funding based on your personal credit score and financial situation; you'll fare much better if you have a good or excellent credit score. In addition, many small business lenders (especially banks) will only work with companies with at least $50,000 or $100,000 of annual revenue and positive monthly cash flow. Other options will cost more interest-wise, but may still give your business the leg up it needs to flourish.

Start with the SBA

The SBA works through traditional banks to help provide loans to small businesses. These will be the lowest-costs loans out there, and there's fierce competition for them. Since the loans are guaranteed by the agency, they come with low interest rates (based on the prime rate) and flexible payment terms that would otherwise be unavailable to small business owners. SBA loan programs include:

- **7(a) loans,** its main loan program, which offers up to $5 million to fund expansions and working capital
- **504 Loans,** which provide up to $5 million to cover land, building, and equipment purchases
- **Microloans,** which offer up to $50,000 for starting a business or providing working capital, equipment, or inventory for an existing business

- **Disaster loans,** which supply up to $2 million for small businesses that have been hurt by natural disasters

You can learn more about SBA loans and start your application process at www.sba.gov.

Microlenders

Microlenders, usually nonprofit organizations, help very small companies with small, short-term loans, even outside the SBA programs. When regular lenders pass on your business because of its size, these lenders step up with funding. Microloans typically top out at $50,000 and come with higher interest rates than bank loans. You'll need to come armed with plenty of proof that your company is worth the risk, including accurate financial statements and a detailed business plan. Along with money, microlenders also often provide free support (like consulting services) to small business owners. Many of these nonprofit lenders offer special loan programs for women and minority business owners. You can find information about microlenders online on sites like *Fit Small Business* (https://.fitsmallbusiness.com) and *NerdWallet* (www.nerdwallet.com).

Online Lenders

A word of caution about online lenders: Loan interest rates can run over 100 percent, meaning you'll have to pay back twice as much as you borrowed. That said, you may be able to find more reasonably priced loans online, particularly if you (or your business) have stellar credit and collateral. There are two main types of online business lenders: peer-to-peer lending (people) and direct lenders (loan companies). Online loans are easier to secure than traditional loans and have quick turnaround times, often supplying funds within 24 hours. Before you sign with an online lender, make sure you fully understand the interest rate and payment terms. You can find information and reviews for online lenders on sites like *The Simple Dollar* (www.thesimpledollar.com) and *ValuePenguin* (www.valuepenguin.com).

How Much Do Small Businesses Borrow?

The average small business loan (in 2018) was $663,000. That covers every type of small business loan all across the US. The average SBA-backed loan was $417,316, and the loans from alternative lenders (not banks) averaged between $50,000 and $80,000.

Invoice Financing and Factoring

If your business is doing well but you have cash flow issues, factoring or financing your accounts receivable invoices (the money your customers owe you but haven't paid yet) may be your best option. Both ways give you a sort of cash advance (usually around 70–85 percent) against invoices you haven't collected yet, but they work slightly differently. With factoring, you essentially turn your accounts receivable over (basically selling them) to the lender, and they deal with all the collections issues; once they collect, they pay your business the remainder of the invoice balances, less their fees. With financing, you keep control over your receivables, including responsibility for collections, then turn the money over to the lender as it comes in. Either way, you'll pay a fee to the lender, usually between 1 and 5 percent, but more if your customers pay late. Reputable companies that factor or finance invoices include BlueVine (www.bluevine.com) and Fundbox (www.fundbox.com).

Chapter 7

Paying Off Debt

If your debt burden is more than you can bear, it's time to do something about it. Choosing debt paydown as your top budget priority is the smartest financial move you can make. You'll earn the big guaranteed returns, more than you'd get from even super successful investments, especially if most of your debt comes with high interest rates (more than 8 percent). To conquer your debt beast, you'll create a plan to funnel any money that's not being used for necessities toward paying off loans. (Note that "necessities" includes retirement savings.) The easiest way to do that is to stop looking at the big picture, your total debt, and focus instead on one debt at a time. That may seem counterintuitive, but going small is the best way to tackle your debt. Put a plan in place, follow it, and you'll be debt-free before you know it.

PRIORITIZE YOUR DEBT

Get Your Debt in Order

The first step toward tackling your debt is prioritizing it. You'll have to balance two important factors here: which debts are essential to your life, and which do the most damage to your net worth. Usually, the most essential and the most damaging debt won't be the same, so these lists will probably look different. Even so, sorting your debts both ways gives you the clearest picture of the best ways to handle your debt.

A reminder: Always make the minimum payment on every debt every month so you don't go into default. When you have your total minimum payment covered, you can turn your attention back to your highest-priority debts for quicker paydown.

PRIORITY: THE MOST ESSENTIAL DEBTS

Your highest priorities on this list include debts that would change your life in a negative way if you didn't pay them. Mortgages and home equity loans usually rank number one here, because if you don't pay those you can lose your house; car loans typically come in second, to avoid repossession. You need somewhere to live and a way to get to work, so these debt payments take top priority all the time, especially when your budget falls short. From there, you'll figure out which other monthly payments *must* be made to keep your life on track.

These Get Top Rank

Using the priority sort order, your highest-ranking debts include:

- Mortgage, home equity loan, HELOC, and rent
- Car loans or leases
- Electricity, gas, water, and phone
- Income and property taxes
- Other secured debts (debts backed by property that can be seized)

Utilities and taxes may not feel like debts, but they are; you owe that money. Having your utilities shut off would make your home unlivable. Skipping tax payments could result in losing your home. Though they're not technically debts, food and medication also rank as top priority, coming before other debt payments and bills.

Further Down in the Rankings

The next debts on this list have medium priority: They won't affect your daily life, but not paying them can lead to much bigger financial problems. Medium priority debts include things like health, homeowner's, and car insurance; student loans; and Internet (this moves up to the highest-priority section if you need the web for work).

Skipping low-priority debts won't affect your life today, but it will impact your long-term financial health. These debts normally come with the highest interest rates as creditors know that they're lower priorities. Debts that count as lower priority include:

- Credit cards
- Merchant accounts
- Medical bills

- Legal bills
- Unsecured personal loans
- Memberships (like gym memberships, for example)

Missing payments on these debts can result in fees and penalties, accumulating interest, and damage to your credit score, but you won't lose your house.

PRIORITY: FINANCIALLY DAMAGING DEBTS

The debts that do the most damage to your net worth and financial health are the ones with the highest interest rates. Usually, these debts are unsecured, meaning they aren't backed by collateral like a house or a car; the creditors have nothing to repossess or foreclose on if you don't pay.

Higher-rate debts are normally linked to consumption, everyday goods and services that were bought with credit rather than cash. Consumables add nothing to your net worth, and the interest charges reduce your net worth, making these types of debts the hardest on your finances.

When you start tackling your debt, you'll want to pay off these high-interest, financially damaging debts first. Priority-wise, you'll rank these debts by their interest rates, from highest to lowest; the amount owed is less important than the interest rate here. Paying these off will save you a lot of money in interest payments that can then be used to pay off less financially damaging debts or put toward building up your net worth.

Get Rid of Toxic Debt ASAP

Debt that comes with especially high interest rates (anything more than 36 percent per year) is toxic and needs to be dealt with as quickly as possible. These debts destroy your current finances and sabotage your financial future. They are extremely hard to pay off even when you always make on-time payments; that's because your payments get applied to interest first, and that interest is shockingly high. In fact, many of these debts are designed to keep you trapped in a financially dangerous borrowing cycle—these creditors do not want you to break free.

Paying off these toxic debts will feel *impossible*, but you can do it. You'll have to make some *temporary* radical budget cutbacks and find ways to increase your income (and maybe get some assistance from family or government), but these *temporary* sacrifices will be worth it. As you pay them off, both your budget and your net worth will benefit, and so will your financial stress levels.

Two More Priorities to Consider

When you're sorting your debts, there are two more factors to consider: the tax implications and your credit score. Mortgages and student loans come with tax breaks to offset their interest costs, setting them lower on the payoff priority list. As for credit, paying down revolving debt (like credit cards) faster bumps up your score because it improves your credit mix (the different kinds of debt you have).

Credit Cards and Minimum Payments

When you make only minimum payments on your credit card bills, you'll be stuck in debt longer and pay thousands more in interest. These payments are designed to drag out your debt so the credit card companies can boost their profits. Making any amount more than the minimum payment (even just $10 or $15 more) every month will reduce the interest you pay over time, and cut that time substantially, as long as you stop using the credit card. The sooner you start increasing the payments, the more money you'll get to keep for yourself.

EFFECTIVE PAYDOWN PLANS

Debt Successfully Conquered!

When you make a plan to pay down your debt, you're already on the path to doing just that. This starts with acknowledging your debt and seeing exactly how much money you owe overall, then quickly pivoting away from that overview and focusing on mechanics. Looking at a whole mountain of debt can be paralyzing. Breaking it into smaller pieces is the only way to get through. That's what your plan will do: cut your debt into more easily manageable slices, then erase them one by one.

SNOWBALL AND AVALANCHE

When it comes to paying down debt, the two most commonly used paydown plans are known as "snowball" and "avalanche." Both focus on paying down one debt at a time, and both will help you dig your way out of debt. With either method, you'll still make on-time payments on all of your other debts, but add extra money to your "focus" debt.

Mathematically speaking, using the avalanche method is a better choice, as you'll reduce the amount you're paying in interest more quickly. Emotionally speaking, the snowball method offers quicker victories, giving you the momentum to keep going. No matter which method you go with, the most important thing to do is to get started. If your chosen method doesn't seem to be working, choose another one as long as you keep going.

Snowball

The snowball debt paydown method calls for paying off your smallest dollar-amount debts first. As you pay off each debt, you add that debt's payment to the next smallest debt to pay that one off faster; the payments "snowball," getting larger over time. Following this plan gives you quicker accomplishments, and that can help you stay on track. Many people gain early success with this method, then switch over to the avalanche method for bigger interest savings.

Avalanche

The avalanche paydown method focuses on your highest-rate debts first. Going in this order helps reduce the overall interest you're paying more quickly. The less interest you're paying, the more of your money will be going toward debt principal. As you cross each higher-rate debt off your list, you'll put the payment from that debt toward the next highest-rate debt until they're all paid off.

Hands Off the 401(k)

When you're looking for extra money to pay down your debt, do not borrow from your 401(k). It's tempting to take out a loan from that big pile of cash but it's a terrible idea for your finances. Most employers won't let you contribute while you have an outstanding 401(k) loan, you'll miss out on the earnings from the money you pulled out, and you have to start paying the loan back with your next paycheck, which can strain your budget even more.

APPLY PAYMENTS TO PRINCIPAL

When you make extra payments toward your debt, you expect it to go straight toward your outstanding principal balance. After all, the whole reason you're making extra payments is to reduce the amount you owe. Unfortunately, it doesn't always work out like that. Different creditors handle extra payments differently, so check in with them before you send in the money.

Some creditors will apply any extra payments to interest first and let any remaining balance go toward principal. One way to work around that is to include your extra payment with your regular payment; that way the regular payment covers the current accrued interest, and the extra payment can go directly toward principal. You can also contact these creditors and ask them how you can make sure extra payments will be applied to principal.

Other creditors automatically apply extra payments to principal. With these creditors, it won't matter if you add more to your regular payment or send in random payments during the month. The exception: If your payment is in the amount of a regular payment, they may just consider it an early payment. To avoid any confusion, make sure to spell out what you're doing:

- Write "apply to principal only" on the memo line of your check
- Check the "extra principal" (or similar language) box on your payment coupon
- Choose "principal reduction" (or similar language) when making an online payment

Whenever you do make extra payments, check back in about a week to make sure they've been applied correctly to your principal balance. If not, contact the creditor and have them correct the mistake.

When You Have More Than One Loan with a Creditor

In some cases, especially with student loans, you may have multiple loans with a single creditor. To make sure the creditor uses your extra payments the way you want them to, you'll have to give them explicit instructions. Otherwise, they'll decide what to do with that extra payment and may even break it up and apply to all of your loans instead of putting it all toward your focus loan.

Contact your creditor or loan servicer to see exactly what they need from you to apply extra payments to your focus loan. You'll probably need to put something in writing (which protects you against erroneous payment application) and send it either by email or regular mail. You can find a good sample letter on the Consumer Financial Protection Bureau (CFPB) website at www .consumerfinance.gov.

If you're paying by check, write "apply to principal" on the memo line. If you're paying online, do it from your loan servicer's website so you have more control over the payment. Check back in a few days to make sure your extra payment was applied correctly. Keep in mind that student loan servicers are *required* to apply payments to outstanding interest before they can apply it to principal.

Making the Final Payment

When you finally get to the point where your next payment will be the last, check in with your creditor to find out the exact payoff amount. For some debts (like credit cards), interest accrues daily, so the balance due changes every day. The creditor will give you a final amount that should be good for a few days; after that, you'll need to ask again. You can make your final payment the same way you'd make any other payment (though some people like to walk into the bank—when applicable—and hand that payment in in person).

Make sure to look at your next statement to make sure the debt is fully paid off and there are no lingering interest charges. Even a tiny remaining balance can build back up quickly if you unknowingly miss a payment and get hit with late charges, which can also hurt your credit score.

GET THE RIGHT HELP

If you start searching for help in your struggle to get out of debt, tons of responses will crop up, but not all of them will be working in your best interests. The right professionals will work with you and help you improve your financial literacy and money management skills. They'll come up with reasonable solutions for paying down your debt and give you solid guidance on things like savings and increasing your credit score. Anyone who asks you to hand everything over to them, promises to "fix" your situation, and seems uninterested in helping you get a handle on your financial situation is not the right help.

FIND A REPUTABLE CREDIT COUNSELOR

If dealing with your debt is more than you can handle on your own, consider working with a credit counselor. Reputable credit counselors will help you create a realistic debt repayment plan and show you ways to avoid taking on any new debt. They work with you to come up with an amount you can realistically afford to pay each month. They will talk with your creditors and get them to accept alternative payment terms that your budget can handle. This often involves extending your loan term, which lowers your monthly payments. Reputable, experienced counselors may be able to help get some of your interest rates (like penalty rates, for example) lowered, get creditors to waive fees, and even put a stop to stressful collection calls.

How to Find a Reputable Credit Counselor

Most trustworthy credit counseling agencies are set up as non-profits. These companies charge very low (sometimes no) fees to help you rebuild your finances in a more positive way. Look for someone who has a solid reputation and a high success rate for helping people get out of debt.

The best credit counselors are trained and certified and will show you their accreditation. You can find reliable, verified information about any credit counseling agencies from the National Foundation for Credit Counseling (NFCC, www.nfcc.org) or the Financial Counseling Association of America (FCAA, www.fcaa.org).

Other good resources include:

- Better Business Bureau (www.bbb.org), which tracks consumer complaints and company responses
- US Department of Justice (www.justice.gov), which provides a list of approved credit counseling agencies
- State attorney general's office (www.naag.org), which collects consumer complaints

Be aware that there are *many* disreputable people who call themselves credit counselors but really just prey on desperate people. Do plenty of research to make sure you're dealing with a reputable company before you hand over any personal information or sign anything. Finding a trustworthy credit counselor will help you reach your financial goals; bad ones leave you worse off than you were before.

Pay Attention to Red Flags

It can sometimes be hard to tell the good guys from the bad guys in the credit counseling universe.

Avoid any companies that:

- Won't send you free information
- Don't disclose their fees up front
- Ask you for money before they'll talk with you
- Promise they'll increase your credit score
- Promise that they can stop pending or potential lawsuits

If you notice even one of these red flags, do not work with that company.

WATCH OUT FOR SCAMS AND BAD IDEAS

Criminals target vulnerable, desperate people, and that includes people who are struggling with debt. They offer "solutions" that sound like the answers to prayers. They're not. Those solutions are scams.

Bad ideas aren't technically illegal, but they will hurt your finances, often for years to come. These bad ideas, which include consolidation loans and debt settlement, sound like good ideas. They're not. Either of these can end up costing you a lot of money, keeping you in debt, and further ruining your credit score.

Companies that offer debt consolidation loans or debt settlement services are in it to make money. Consolidation companies roll your current debts into one giant debt with an extended payback period, tack on often-hidden fees (they just add the fees to the amount you owe), and frequently increase the interest rate over time. Any one of these would increase the total cost of your debt; all three together increase it substantially. Debt settlement also has a negative effect on your finances. Here, the company "negotiates" with your creditors to reduce your debt balances, but often charge very high fees (like 20 percent of your debt), which has the effect of increasing the amount you owe. On top of that, debt settlement hurts your credit score, and you may owe income taxes on the amount of debt your creditors "forgive." Finally, there are a *lot* of fraudulent debt consolidation and debt settlement companies out there. If you still decide to go this route proceed with extreme caution.

Protect yourself and your financial future by clearing up your debt the right way. There's no quick and easy answer. It takes time, effort, and discipline to fix this problem, and you just have to work your way through it.

Credit Repair Scams

If someone says that you can improve your credit score overnight, it's a scam. Repairing poor credit isn't quick and easy. Anyone who promises you that it can be is lying.

Avoid working with anyone who offers up any of these as a poor-credit solution:

- Starting over with a new Social Security number, which is illegal
- Giving you a new "credit identity" and a credit profile number (CPN), which is illegal
- Removing negative but true information (such as bankruptcies) from your credit report, which is illegal
- Guaranteeing a fixed increase (like 200 points) in your credit score, which is a lie

You'll also want to avoid working with anyone who discourages you from reading a contract before you sign it, even if they do it in a friendly way ("Don't worry about that, it's just standard legal language," for example).

The truth: The only way to repair poor credit and increase your credit score is by paying down your debt and developing good financial habits. Anyone who tells you otherwise is scamming you.

Be Wary of Consolidation Loans

Steer clear of debt consolidation companies that contact you rather than the other way around. These unscrupulous "finance companies" can end up increasing your debt load through high interest rates, disguised fees, and hidden collateral clauses that put your home or other assets at risk.

Avoid Debt Settlement Companies

Debt settlement companies may be able to make part of your debt disappear, but they won't do anything to improve your financial situation. In fact, they may make it worse. These companies say they'll contact your creditors to negotiate on your behalf and settle your debts for less money. What they often don't tell you:

- You may have to make a large one-time payment to completely pay off the reduced debt
- Settling debt claims for less hurts your credit score and makes it harder to borrow money in the future
- You may owe income taxes on the forgiven portion of the debt

There are also a lot of scam artists in this space. If a debt settlement company tells you to stop making payments to your creditors, advises you to stop contacting creditors on your own, or requires upfront cash from you before they get started, walk away. No legitimate company will ever tell you to do any of those things.

DEALING WITH COLLECTIONS

Stop Calling Me!

Debt collectors prey on all of the negative feelings you have about being in debt, making even people with good credit histories feel like criminals and deadbeats. All they care about is meeting their quotas, and many don't care how they do that or even if a debt is legitimately yours. Collectors run the spectrum from irritating to predatory, and some even dip into illegal practices. It's vitally important that you know your rights, verify these debts, and take control of the situation away from the collector. That way, if the debt really is yours, you can figure out the best way to handle it with minimal financial and credit-related consequences.

THE RIGHT WAY TO RESPOND (IT'S *NOT* PAYING)

When you get a call or a letter from a debt collector, your instincts will probably tell you to either respond or ignore it. Both of those options are mistakes and can come back around to hurt you. If you communicate at all with the collector about the debt or if you pay *any amount* (even $5) toward the debt, you have officially acknowledged the debt. If you ignore every communication, which may include court summons, you could end up with a judgment against you that allows the collector to garnish your wages.

The right way to handle collections is to start by requesting a validation letter, which they must provide within five business days of the first contact. That letter must include full details on the debt, complete contact information for the collections company, and an explanation of how you can challenge the debt.

Verify the Debt

Collectors may have incorrect information. Collectors also may lie (there are many scammers in this space). Demand proof of the debt they're trying to collect, and make sure it is both legitimately yours and correct. Once you've asked them to verify the debt, they have to leave you alone until they provide the information you requested. If they don't send you proof of the debt, you can demand that they stop contacting you with a cease and desist letter.

If it really is your debt, find your records from the original creditor (whoever you owed the money to initially) along with proof of any payments you made. You can use this information to help negotiate a settlement or payment plan if you can't pay the debt in full right away.

If the debt isn't yours or isn't 100 percent correct, dispute it. If you challenge the claim within thirty days of the collector's first contact, they must stop asking for payment until the dispute has been settled. If you file the challenge after that thirty days is up, they can keep contacting you during the investigation period.

Record or Document *Everything*

Any time you communicate with the debt collector, keep a full record. Keep copies of everything you send to them, and only send written communications through certified mail (so you have proof they received it). When you speak with them, either record the call (with their knowledge) or take detailed notes during the conversation. Document the date and time of the call, the collector's name, and everything you discuss.

Be very careful what you say to them. They will use anything you say to help them collect. Don't talk with them about your paycheck, your budget, or other bills you have to pay. Keep the conversation focused on the specific debt they're collecting, but do not accept responsibility for the debt until you have verified that it's real and correct.

Get Help from the CFPB

The Consumer Financial Protection Bureau provides information and resources to help you deal with debt collectors. That includes sample letters you can use to respond to the collector, information about your rights, and links to submit complaints about the collector's tactics or fraudulent claims. Visit the CFPB website at www.consumerfinance.gov.

KNOW THE RULES

You have rights. A special law, the Fair Debt Collection Practices Act (FDCPA), is there to protect you from predatory and overzealous collectors. The FDCPA puts limits on when collectors can contact you, how they can speak to you, and who else they can contact. Get familiar with its key provisions, and use the law to stand up to collectors who are giving you a hard time.

What Collectors Cannot Do

Debt collectors may act forcefully and try to intimidate you, but there's a legal limit on what they're actually allowed to do. Among other things, debt collectors are not allowed to:

- Curse at you
- Threaten you with violence or arrest
- Harass or bully you
- Lie to you about who they are or what you owe
- Call you before 8:00 a.m. or after 9:00 p.m.
- Call you at work if you tell them your employer doesn't allow this type of call
- Call you at a specific time if you've told them that time is inconvenient
- Call you at all if you ask them *in writing* to stop calling

If a collector does any of those things, file a complaint immediately with the FTC (www.ftc.gov) or the CFPB (www.consumerfinance.gov).

Contacting Other People

Collectors can and do contact other people in your life, but they're only allowed to contact them one time and for specific reasons. They are allowed to contact friends, family, and employers for your contact information if the collector is unable to locate you. They can also call your employer to verify employment. However, they are not allowed to reveal that they are debt collectors or the reason they're trying to contact you.

The Statute of Limitations

Collections come with a deadline known as the statute of limitations. The debt is only legally enforceable during that time period; once the deadline passes, it becomes practically impossible for the collector to win a judgment against you in court. Collectors know they're on the clock, which is one reason they pursue debts so aggressively. The clock starts with the last activity on the debt in question and stops based on a combination of state law and type of debt. If you make a payment (any size) or admit to owing the debt, though, you might restart the statute of limitations. Know where your debt falls in this cycle before you engage with the collector; it can give you a leg up in negotiations.

The other time issue has to do with credit reporting. There's a limit to how long a debt will be listed on your credit report. If the debt has already come off, or will be coming off soon, that also strengthens your bargaining position with the collector.

NEGOTIATE WITH THE DEBT COLLECTOR

After you've verified that a debt is yours, the next step is figuring out how to pay it. Look at your budget to see how much you can afford to put toward this debt. If you can't pay the full amount all at once, you may be able to split it up into three or four payments.

Debt collectors act fast and generally will not agree to payment plans longer than four months. They also want to collect as much as they can, but they are open to negotiation, especially if time is running out for collection.

When you know how much you can pay and how you can do it (lump sum or a few payments), you can make an offer to the collector, but start with a number that's a little lower than you can afford. For example, if you can afford to pay $3,500 against a $5,000 debt, you might offer to pay $3,000. The collector will probably make a counteroffer that's higher than yours, possibly for the full debt. Stick with your plan, and don't agree to more than you can afford to pay.

Once you've come to an agreement:

- Get it in writing before you make any payment
- Make sure the written agreement clearly states that the full debt will be settled when the agreed-upon amount is paid in full
- Be aware that the statute of limitations restarts as soon as you make a payment
- Pay your debt in accordance with the terms you've agreed to

Another important factor to consider: tax consequences. If the collector cancels more than $600 of debt, they will report that to the IRS. You'll get a special Form 1099-C at tax time and will have to report the canceled debt as income and pay tax on it.

UNDERSTAND BANKRUPTCY

Bringing Your Debt to Court

When you're drowning in debt, it may seem like filing for bankruptcy protection is the only way out. For many people, though, this choice can do more damage to their future finances than working through their financial setbacks. Plus, depending on the specifics of your situation, you may not qualify for bankruptcy filing. Before you undertake a bankruptcy filing, it's crucial to understand the different kinds of bankruptcy and how they work, along with the severe impact filing can have on your financial future.

IF YOU'RE CONSIDERING BANKRUPTCY

Many people think of bankruptcy as a financial do-over, where all of their debts get wiped out and they have a fresh, clean credit slate. That's not true. Here are seven things you need to know about bankruptcy before you make this major financial move:

1. If you file under chapter 7 (more on that in the next section), you can lose your house.
2. Some debts are nondischargeable (meaning you'll still owe the full amount), including taxes, child support and alimony, student loans, and court fines or penalties.
3. Bankruptcy filings are public, which means anyone can look up that information.

4. Creditors can (and usually do) turn to your cosigners for debts that get discharged under your bankruptcy; the discharge is specific to you, not the debt.

5. You normally need permission to spend any of your own money once you file chapter 13 bankruptcy.

6. Bankruptcy may not stop creditors from repossessing property used as collateral to secure a debt (such as the car securing your car loan).

7. Your credit score will decrease dramatically once you file for bankruptcy, and the bankruptcy can stay on your credit report for up to ten years.

Before you settle on bankruptcy, explore your alternatives. Find a reputable credit counselor and discuss your situation to see if there's another way to deal with your debt outside the court system. You can find a listing of reliable credit counselors on the US Department of Justice website (www.justice.gov).

UNDERSTAND THE TWO TYPES OF BANKRUPTCY

Individuals can file for two types of bankruptcy: chapter 7 and chapter 13. In some cases, only one of those options will be available to you. If you do have a choice, it's important to carefully weigh the pros and cons of each before you decide which form will work better for your situation. Your decision will come down to the types of debt you have, whether you want to hold on to specific assets, and your total monthly income. Filing for either form of bankruptcy will damage your credit score and history, but it can have a smaller impact than not filing and allowing more debts to fall into delinquency and default.

Chapter 7

Chapter 7 bankruptcy (also called "straight" bankruptcy) gets rid of most or all of your debts within six months. To start the process, you petition the court by filling out a lot of paperwork, which is available for free download on the US Courts website (www.uscourts.gov). That paperwork provides a detailed look at your finances based on information from pay stubs, bank statements, credit card statements, loan documents, and a listing of all of your assets and liabilities. Once that's all complete, you'll file the documents along with a $335 filing fee to the bankruptcy court. If you use an attorney (probably a good idea), the fees run between $1,500 and $5,000.

Next, you'll have to turn over your assets (except for exempt assets) and liabilities to a trustee of the court. The trustee will usually sell off your assets and use the proceeds to make payments to your creditors. Exempt assets (the stuff you're allowed to keep) may include:

- Cars
- Clothing
- Household furnishings and appliances
- Retirement savings and pensions
- Some of the equity in your home

What you can keep varies by state and depends on the value of the assets.

Chapter 13

A chapter 13 bankruptcy works more like a financial fix up that includes a three-to-five-year repayment plan. Unlike chapter 7, most debts don't get canceled under chapter 13, but that can be beneficial for someone who might lose their car or other assets under chapter 7. You don't turn over your property to a trustee here; rather, you develop and stick with an extended debt payment plan. Along with property, this version also protects cosigners.

Working through a chapter 13 bankruptcy isn't easy, but it can help you develop stronger money management skills. Payments are based on your disposable income, all money you have coming in from all sources minus absolutely necessary living expenses. At the end of the payment period, as long as you have made all of your monthly payments, any unsecured debts (like credit card debt) that remain will be fully discharged. The filing fee for chapter 13 is $310, and attorney fees average around $2,000.

For More Complete Information

You can find reliable and detailed information about filing for bankruptcy, including forms to file and step-by-step instructions on how to file online, at www.nolo.com. Other good sources of information include the Federal Trade Commission (www.consumer.ftc.gov) and *The Balance* (www.thebalance .com).

Chapter 8

Living Debt-Free
(Doesn't Mean *No* Borrowing)

There's a small distinction between borrowing money and being in debt. When you think about these two terms differently, you can use borrowing to your advantage without ending up in debt. In this context, *borrowing* refers to using someone else's money to improve your financial situation. You can build your net worth, build your credit, improve your cash flow, or all three. Being in debt comes with a more negative twist, as it benefits your creditors while hurting your financial situation. Paying off your debt provides you with extra opportunities for saving and investing.

WEALTH BUILDING

Your Own Golden-Egg Goose

When you have a lot of debt, too much of your money goes toward interest payments, and that interest expense reduces your net worth. Once your debt is paid off, you can funnel all of that money toward building your own fortune, then watch it grow. Wealth doesn't come overnight, and it takes careful planning to make it happen. That includes addressing poor spending habits, creating additional income, and staying out of debt. But building true wealth often also involves borrowing. You can live debt-free and still borrow money wisely, on your own terms, to further your own path to wealth.

CUT CREDIT SPENDING
TO BOOST SAVINGS

Never spend more than you earn. That's the number one rule of personal finance and the only way to achieve financial security and independence. It's also the first step on the path toward building wealth for two very important reasons. First, any money you don't spend increases your savings and the money available for investment. Second, spending more than you earn requires borrowing, the kind of borrowing that builds debt instead of wealth. Spending money mindfully, which means you're aware of what you're buying and how much it costs both in terms of money and opportunity, allows you to buy what you really want without depleting your net worth.

It's Not about Skipping Lattes

Mindful spending is not about depriving yourself; it's about consciously deciding which purchases are important to you and buying only those things. If you grabbing an $8 mocha latte every morning is one of the best parts of your day, that's $8 worth spending as long as you can afford it. If a daily latte isn't worth as much to you as having an extra $2,920 at the end of the year ($8 × 365 days), stop buying them.

You know what's important to you and what brings joy or purpose to your day. Money you're spending for things that don't add value to your life are not worthwhile, and those are the costs to identify and cut.

The Extra Cost of Credit Card Spending

If you put $8 on a credit card every day for one month, you'd end up with a $240 balance. Assuming a 15 percent APR on your card, if you make only minimum payments, it will take more than two years and cost almost $50 in interest to pay off that balance. That means the $8 daily expense really cost more than $9.60 every day. It may not seem like much, but over time that extra cost adds up to thousands of dollars that could have been put toward your wealth.

If you had put that money to work for you instead, even just in a high-yield savings account, you would have earned rather than lost money. Putting that $240 in a savings account earning 2 percent would have given you $244 at the end of the year. Doesn't seem like much, but compared to a negative $290 ($240 spent plus $50 interest), the real difference to your net worth is $534.

SMART BORROWING BOOSTS
NET WORTH

The key to smart borrowing is simple: Earn more with the borrowed money than you're paying in interest. That can be as simple as paying off credit card balances every month while earning rewards points; any reward minus zero interest counts as a gain for you. Or it could mean a mortgage on a rental property where the rent more than covers the monthly expenses. When you earn more than you're paying, the difference increases your net worth.

Again, going into this borrowing with a well-thought-out plan makes all the difference. If, for example, you don't pay off that credit card balance in full, you'll pay more in interest than you earn in rewards, which decreases your net worth. If you borrow too much money at too high of a rate for a rental property, and the rent can't cover even the mortgage payment, your net worth will take a hit.

A smart borrowing plan calls for:

- An excellent credit score
- Ample incoming cash flow
- Plenty of savings to cover unexpected expenses
- Mindful purchasing
- Reasonable expectation of profits on the deal

For smaller forays into borrowing to earn, you can run the numbers yourself. For example, take your monthly budget and cash flow into account before buying $4,500 worth of living room furniture with zero percent financing for six months (which calls for payments of $750 per month). Other endeavors, like buying your first rental property, call for help from experienced professionals. Yes, their fees will eat into your profits, but you're less likely to profit without their expertise, and they can help you figure out the optimal amount to borrow and still come out ahead.

Net Worth Can Be Negative

Don't be shocked or dismayed if your net worth is negative. That's a function of being in debt and not having a lot of assets, very common for the under-forty crowd. As you pay off debt and build wealth, your net worth will swing from negative to positive, and from there to stellar.

FASTER RETIREMENT SAVINGS

A Savings Spree

Once your budget stops being dragged down by debt (especially high-interest debt), you can focus on creating a retirement nest egg. Now you'll be able to build up retirement savings at a much faster clip or start saving if you haven't been able to before. All the money that was directed toward debt can now be put toward building wealth and securing a comfortable financial future.

MAXIMIZE RETIREMENT CONTRIBUTIONS

If your focus on debt has kept you from contributing the maximum to retirement savings, now is the time to change that. If you have access to a retirement savings plan through your employer, start participating as soon as possible and contributing the maximum amount allowable. If you don't have access to an employer plan, you can open up and fund your own retirement savings account at any bank or brokerage firm; it takes less than thirty minutes to do this online. Depending on your income level, you may be able to fully fund both an employer retirement account and an individual retirement account (IRA) to supersize your savings.

Maximum contribution limits change every year. You can find out this year's maximum by visiting the IRS website at www.irs.gov.

Move Retirement Savings to the Front Burner

Millions of Americans have been forced to delay retirement savings in order to make debt payments. A study (by Nationwide Insurance) found that 61 percent of employees say that debt gets in the way of retirement savings. Overall, student loans top the savings impediment list, followed closely by credit card debt. In fact, a study by TIAA found that:

- Eighty-four percent of Americans have student debt that prevents them from saving enough for retirement
- Seventy-three percent of people with student loans say they've either stopped contributing or contribute less than the maximum to their retirement accounts
- Twenty-six percent of Americans who haven't yet opened retirement accounts cite student debt as the reason

As soon as your debt is paid off, retirement savings should jump to the head of the list of financial priorities. The sooner you can get started, the more financially comfortable your retirement will be.

Get Free Money from Your Employer

If your employer offers a retirement savings plan, like a 401(k) or 403(b) plan, and offers matching contributions, get them. All you have to do to get this free money is put some of your own money into retirement savings, and if you don't take advantage of this, you are actually walking away from *free money.*

Here's how an employer match works: When you contribute money to your retirement account, your employer puts in extra money to match it. For example, many employers offer a 3 percent match (meaning they'll match up to 3 percent of your salary) as an extra benefit. If you earn $60,000 per year, your employer would add up to $1,800 ($60,000 × 0.03) to your retirement account as long as you contribute that much yourself. If you contributed only $1,000, they would match your $1,000, and you would lose that extra $800 of free money. If you haven't been contributing at least the matching amount to your retirement savings because you were focused on paying off debt (or for any other reason), contact your employer and ramp up your contribution today.

MAKE COMPOUNDING WORK FOR YOU

When you have debt, compounding works against you. Along with the interest you pay on the original amount of principal you borrowed, you may also be paying interest on previously accumulated interest. The longer you owe, the more interest you pay. That increases your total debt and the total amount of interest you pay over the life of your debt.

When you switch budget gears from debt paydown to savings buildup, the compounding equation does a backflip. Now your money begins to go to work for you, speeding up wealth accumulation.

When you're trying to build substantial retirement savings, time is your best friend (the exact opposite of when you're paying down debt). The more time you have on your side, the bigger your savings will grow. What's more, it will keep growing even if you stop contributing to it, thanks to the power of compounding.

Here's how compounding works (with totally made-up numbers): You put $1,000 into your retirement account and it earns $50 in one year (a 5 percent earnings rate). Now you have $1,050 and your money earns $52.50 for the year. After two years, your account balance is $1,102.50 even though you never made another contribution (but it will grow even faster if you do). As the balance grows, your account will earn more, and your retirement fund will snowball all on its own.

Catch Up with Your Retirement Savings

If you're at least fifty years old, the IRS lets you make special "catch-up" contributions to your retirement accounts every year. These extra contributions are available with both employer-sponsored and individual retirement accounts. And if you're allowed to contribute to both types of accounts, you may be able to catch up in both. Visit www.irs.gov to find out whether and how much extra you can contribute.

MAINTAIN AN EXCELLENT CREDIT SCORE

Keep Your Numbers Up

An excellent credit score unlocks many financial advantages. That comes with a catch: In order to have a great credit score, you have to use credit. When you've finally managed to pay off your debt, the thought of borrowing anything can seem like a land mine. However, building up and maintaining a strong credit score depends on responsible borrowing. When you use no credit at all, your credit score will decline. That can be a problem even if you plan to never borrow money again, because your credit score can affect your ability to get a job, rent an apartment, and get life insurance (among other things). You can carefully borrow just enough to keep your credit score in the green zone without going into debt.

THE BENEFITS OF GOOD CREDIT

Qualifying for lower interest rates every time you borrow money is the number one benefit of a good credit score, but it's not the only advantage a strong score offers. Your credit score offers one-glance information about your likelihood to pay back debt; a higher score means you're a better payer and pose less risk to the lender. When you're considered a safe bet, you'll gain an edge when there's competition for loans, rental apartments, and even jobs. Just like a poor credit score can drag you down, an excellent credit score can open doors.

How Much Do Rates Really Matter?

The difference between paying 3.75 percent and 4.50 percent interest may not seem like much, but that tiny difference could add up to thousands of dollars over time. Consider this: If you had a $200,000 thirty-year mortgage at 3.75 percent, you'd have monthly payments of $926 and you'd pay around $133,000 in interest over the life of your loan. That same loan with a rate of 4.50 percent would result in monthly payments of $1,013 and more than $165,000 in total interest paid. In real numbers, a better credit score could save you nearly $100 every month and more than $30,000 over time.

Good versus Poor Score

According to ValuePenguin (2019), someone with an excellent credit score (over 720) will pay no more than 12.5 percent interest on a personal loan and an average of 3.6 percent on a car loan. Compare that to someone with poor credit (below 640), who gets hit with a rate of up to 32.0 percent on personal loans and at least 9.72 percent on car loans.

Other Ways Good Credit Helps You

When you have an exceptional credit score (over 800), lenders will want to work with you. They'll offer speedy approvals and better terms to get you to borrow from them. They'll flood you with offers for premium credit cards and low-interest loans, putting you in the driver's seat when you do want to borrow money. But the benefits of a great credit score don't stop there. Other advantages include:

- Special credit card perks, like access to private airport lounges or supercharged rewards deals (such as earning two points for every dollar you spend instead of the usual one)
- Fast and easy approval for rental properties; when landlords are flooded with applications, yours moves to the top of the pile
- Lower car insurance premiums (when compared to someone with the same other circumstances but a lower credit score)
- No need for security deposits on utility accounts and cell phone contracts
- Sign-up bonuses or deep discounts when you open a new credit account

MAINTAIN YOUR CREDIT WISELY

You can keep your credit score in the green-light zone without getting buried in debt and without paying any interest. Using a credit card or two for some regular expenses, then paying the balance(s) in full every month keeps your credit history in great shape without incurring any interest expenses or finance charges. If you're concerned about running up debt, here are some steps you can take to make sure that doesn't happen:

- Use a credit card only for something that you can afford to pay for with cash you already have.
- Any time you use a credit card, immediately set aside the same amount of cash so it will be available when it's time to pay the bill.
- Limit your utilization to 15 percent or less of your available balance.

- Check your credit card balance regularly so you can stay on top of how much you owe (especially if other people, like a spouse or child, are also using the same account).
- Pay all credit card bills in full every month.
- If you can't pay off the bill in one month, stop using credit cards immediately and until the balance is back to zero.

You can use a budgeting app like Mint or Mvelopes to track your credit card spending and make sure you have enough cash on hand to cover everything you're charging.

REWARDS CARDS/CREDIT CARD ADVANTAGES

They'll Pay You to Borrow Money

When you use credit cards the right way, you can actually make money on the deal. Most credit card companies offer built-in consumer protections and insurance benefits. Many also offer spending rewards in the form of miles, points, or cash back. They do this so you'll use your card more in the hopes that you'll pay them a lot of interest. But you can use your card all the time, rack up rewards, and never pay them an extra dime.

Of course, credit card companies do their best to discourage this type of savvy spending management, but you don't have to fall for their traps. Watch your spending, pay your balance(s) in full every month, and the credit card company will be paying you to use their card.

THE SMART WAY TO EARN REWARDS

To make money by using your credit cards, you must pay the balances in full every month, on time. The moment you're paying interest, you're losing money on the deal. This strategy does not work if you have credit card debt or run a balance. In fact, it will lead to you losing even more money to interest payments. But when you don't run a balance, you pay zero interest, and the credit card company pays you to use their card.

That consistent payment habit also boosts your credit score, which can increase your earnings here. When you have an excellent credit score, you may be able to earn rewards at a much faster clip for an even bigger profit.

Don't Spend More to Score Rewards

The drive to earn rewards can lead to overspending. Don't let it. Never spend more than you've planned just to get more rewards. Credit card companies will try to lure you into extra spending by offering double points or higher percentage cash back on specific purchases (like restaurant dinners) or if you use specific vendors (like hotels or high-end shops). Never buy anything you wouldn't otherwise buy, and don't spend more than you've budgeted just to get the extra points. Stick with your regular plan, and the points will accumulate.

Bored with the Same Old Rewards?

You don't have to be stuck with standard credit card rewards that you won't use. You can find cards that offer different options such as Uber or Airbnb credits, free in-flight Wi-Fi, or access to presale tickets for concerts and events.

Take Advantage of Special Redemptions

Many credit card companies have dedicated "malls" on their websites that allow you to redeem points for goods and gift cards. When you use your points to buy from preferred partners, you can score discounts on top of the free money. For example, you could get a $50 gift card for $40 worth of points, making an even bigger profit on the deal. They may also offer great deals on particular products or travel and hotel stays that you book through them. Check the card issuer's website regularly to take advantage of the best deals for you.

USE EVERY FREE ADVANTAGE OF YOUR CREDIT CARDS

Along with rewards, using your credit card for certain purchases can come with special benefits. Different cards have different programs, so check your user agreement or look on the card issuer's website to find out all of the benefits your cards offer. Common benefits include:

- Insurance on rental cars
- Extended warranties
- Price protection (when you buy something and the price drops the next day, the credit card company may refund you the difference)
- Free foreign transactions (so you don't have to pay extra fees when you make purchases using foreign currencies)
- Replacement insurance (if something you buy breaks or gets lost or stolen within a set time period, usually thirty days)
- Travel insurance
- Fraud protection

Taking advantage of these freebies can save you thousands of dollars, and that's in addition to any rewards you earn for using the card.

INVESTING (IN PROPERTIES, ETC.) BUT NOT GAMBLING (MARGIN ACCOUNTS)

May the Odds Be with You

Though they have a few things in common (such as risk), investing and gambling are not the same. Gambling comes with a short-term (sometimes immediate) result, relies on luck, and is more likely to result in losses than winnings. Investing has a long-term focus, backed by research, with the intent to produce income and gains over time. That's not to say that investments never lose money; they do. But investment losses can be mitigated much more easily than gambling losses, and you can take specific steps to minimize the risks.

THE SMART WAY TO INVEST WITH BORROWED MONEY

The term "leverage" means using borrowed funds to invest in assets or projects to increase potential returns. This also comes with extra downside risk if the investment doesn't do as well as expected (leverage can increase losses and gains). You can use leverage to invest in anything from real estate to a small business to stocks and bonds. However, the only time it really makes sense to invest with borrowed money is when the investment is expected to return more than the cost of the loan before the loan comes due. Even then, if the investment performs poorly, the losses will be bigger than if you'd invested without borrowing, so use this strategy cautiously and only in situations that come with relatively low risk and high potential earnings.

Choose Investments Carefully

When you're borrowing money to invest, you want to make sure you're investing in something that will almost certainly turn a profit after taking the loan into account. Look to lower-risk assets, like real estate, and avoid high-risk assets, like speculative stocks. Along with any standard due diligence practices you use for regular investing, add another layer that looks at both the upside and downside potential of investing with borrowed funds. Compare the costs of the loans to the most conservative returns (the least amount you think the investment will earn) to see if you'll still end up with a profit. For example, if you realistically expect the investment to earn 6 to 10 percent returns over time, make your comparison using the 6 percent scenario. If you aren't sure how to figure out whether it makes sense to borrow money to buy a particular investment, either consult a trusted professional with related experience or don't borrow the money.

Focus On the Costs

The interest rate on your borrowed funds has a direct bearing on profit potential, so you want to qualify for the lowest possible rates. That can be done with a combination of strong credit and a large amount of equity (assets in a margin account, down payment on a rental property). When you're willing and able to secure a large portion of the investment with your own funds, you're less likely to walk away if the deal turns sour; the more you're invested, the more secure your lender will feel. Since interest rates are based on risk, the less risk you present, the lower your interest rate will be. Minimizing this expense results in a higher level of profitability (or smaller loss) for your investment.

More Expensive to
Finance Investment Properties

Real estate investment loans come with higher rates than other mortgages, even though both have secured assets in play. Borrowing money for a rental property that you will not live in (as opposed to an owner-occupied rental) costs more than borrowing money for your primary home, both in interest and loan fees. Conventional mortgage lenders offer the best deals, making them the best choice for your investment property.

DON'T GAMBLE WITH
BORROWED MONEY

You may be tempted to use leverage to rapidly increase your investment holdings, but that strategy—known as margin investing—comes with an enormous helping of risk. You're essentially gambling, and the odds won't be in your favor. While margin trading can boost your investment profit potential substantially, it has at least as much (sometimes more) loss potential.

In order to do this, you need to open a margin account with your broker. The legal requirement for margin borrowing is 50 percent, meaning you have to fund your account with at least half of the cash for the purchase. This strategy effectively doubles your buying power but can also leave you in dire financial straits if the investment tanks.

Day Trading Is a Mash-Up

Day trading adds a huge helping of gambling to investing. It's all about betting on market movements and momentary price discrepancies rather than the actual value of investments. Day traders do research and math so they're not quite gamblers, but they aren't investors either.

How Margin Investing Works

Investing on margin means that you're borrowing money from your brokerage to buy stocks or other securities. Here's how that works: Let's say you have $5,000 in your brokerage account but want to buy $10,000 worth of stock. You borrow the other $5,000 from your broker and buy the stock, which acts as collateral for the loan. Now you have $10,000 worth of stock in your account and owe your broker $5,000; your equity is $5,000, or 50 percent of the account.

If the stock increases in value to $15,000, you get to keep $10,000 for a 100 percent return on *your* investment (it's a 50 percent return on the investment as a whole). That's how margin investing can supersize your profits.

If the investment value drops, you end up with a loss and you still have to pay back the loan with interest. There's generally no time limit on margin loans, which can give the share price a chance to rebound, but you do have to pay interest the whole time they're outstanding, which chips away at your profits and increases losses.

The Danger of Margin Investing

When you invest in stocks, there's always the risk that you'll lose the entire amount of money you invested. When you invest on margin, you face the risk of losing *more* than your original investment. For example, imagine that $10,000 stock investment became worthless (an extreme example). You lost your whole $5,000 investment and you also have to pay back the $5,000 loan plus interest, bringing your total losses to more than $10,000.

A more likely scenario involves a large partial loss. The value may drop enough that your equity falls below the broker's maintenance margin requirement (usually 30 or 40 percent), the minimum equity allowed in the margin account. Here's what that looks like: With a 40 percent maintenance margin, your equity would have to stay above $4,000 (0.40 × $10,000). If the value of the stocks in the account fell to $8,000, your equity would fall to $3,000 ($8,000 - $5,000), below the maintenance margin. When that happens, your broker may issue a *margin call*, which means you have to immediately bring your equity up by $1,000 by adding either cash or securities to the account. If you don't do that, the broker will sell your investment and collect their money. You can learn more about margin investing from Financial Industry Regulatory Authority (FINRA) at www.finra.org.

Chapter 9

The Other Side of Debt/Be the Bank

Most of us are familiar with the borrower side of debt: We borrow money and pay it back over time with interest. The other side seems reserved for big banks and other financial institutions, but you can also benefit from the lending side of debt. When you act as a lender, the debt script gets flipped: You're the one collecting interest and making money on the deal. You benefit from the positive cash flow of fixed income and more stable principal (compared to stocks). This side of debt increases your net worth rather than depleting it.

INVESTING IN DEBT

Be the Bank

When you invest in debt, you're either directly or indirectly lending money, just as if you were a bank. The goal is to earn steady fixed income for a long period of time, but there's no guarantee you'll enjoy that outcome. Before you dive into debt investing, learn everything you can about the potential risks and how to minimize them. Like all other investments, taking bigger risks can score you bigger rewards, here in the form of higher interest rates. Just remember the reasons behind those huge potential returns, and do your due diligence so you don't take the wrong risk and demolish your savings.

THE BANK (ALMOST) ALWAYS WINS

Like all investing, debt investing comes with risk. But as the bank (lender), there's a lot you can do to minimize your risk and maximize both your earnings and cash flow. Since you are lending the money, you have more control over the terms. You get to decide who borrows from you (and who doesn't). Banks also protect their capital by spreading out their risk over multiple (thousands or more) loans; they never put all of their lending eggs in a single borrower's basket.

Collecting Interest

When you're on the lending side of debt, you're the one who collects interest rather than paying it. Instead of eating away at your budget, here interest feeds your budget and increases your available cash flow.

In most cases, that interest constitutes taxable income (the exception is interest earned on municipal bonds). Unlike with a paycheck, taxes don't come out of your interest payments, and that means you'll have to make the payments yourself. If your interest earnings will be significant, you may need to make quarterly estimated tax payments to avoid penalties at tax time. Your tax accountant can help you work through the numbers and figure out the best way to manage any tax bill.

Estimated Tax Payments

If your investment income will come with a tax bill of more than $1,000 (meaning you'll owe at least that much when you file your income taxes), you'll need to make estimated tax payments throughout the year or risk getting hit with tax penalties and interest. You can find an estimated tax worksheet and filing instructions on the IRS website at www.irs.gov.

Working with Safety Nets

Institutional lenders work with safety nets to minimize their risk of loss whenever they make loans. The two main safety nets used are collateral and cosigners, and both protect the lender if the primary borrower does not pay back their loan.

Collateral is physical property (like real estate or a car) that's used to secure a loan; if the borrower doesn't pay the money back, the lender gets the property. While collateral is usually pegged to a related loan (a car loan is secured by the car being purchased, for example), it doesn't have to be. Lenders can require collateral on personal loans as well.

Cosigners are people who agree to pay a loan if the main borrower defaults (stops making payments). Though many don't realize it, cosigners are 100 percent responsible for the full loan balance plus interest. When lenders can't collect from the primary borrower, they'll shift their collection efforts to the cosigner. This safety net is normally used when the main borrower has no or limited credit history or a poor credit score, and the cosigner has strong credit.

KNOW THE RISKS

Debt investing comes with its own set of risks, different from the risks of equity investing. While many people believe debt securities are less risky than equity securities (like stocks), that's not always true. In fact, some types of debt investing are at least as risky as—and sometimes more risky than—aggressive stock investments.

Whenever you lend money, there's a chance you won't be paid back; that's called default risk, and most lenders are well aware of it. There's another risk that novice lenders may not think about: interest rate risk, and it's an equally important consideration if you're getting into the lending game. You'll also have to contend with liquidity risk, which speaks to a more limited ability to quickly convert investments into cash.

Interest Rate Risk

Debt investments lose value when interest rates rise. That phenomenon is referred to as interest rate risk: the chance that prevailing interest rates will rise, and you'll be unable to take advantage of the increase because your money is already tied up in a lower-rate debt security. If you try to sell your lower-rate securities, they'll fetch lower prices, leaving you with less free cash to devote to newer, higher-rate investments. This risk works in tandem with inflation risk, the chance that inflation will outpace your investment earnings, effectively negating them.

Default Risk

When someone doesn't pay you back, that's called default, and it's extremely common. While you can mitigate default risk with due diligence, credit checks, and collateral, you can't eliminate it entirely unless you stick strictly with fully guaranteed debt securities. That means US Treasury bonds, the safest possible debt investments, and they trade reduced risk for extremely low interest rates (less than high-yield savings accounts as of August 2019).

Liquidity Risk

In investment terms, liquidity refers to the ability to quickly exchange securities for cash. Stocks and exchange-traded funds (ETFs), for example, are highly liquid because you can sell them at any time and collect cash (though not necessarily as much cash as you want). Real estate is illiquid, because it takes a long time to sell and settle. Debt investments fall somewhere between the two, depending on the type of debt. Many debt investments involve long periods of time during which you can't get your money back easily. If you might need cash soon, don't invest that money in illiquid debt investments (like peer-to-peer lending or hard money lending).

BUY BONDS

Bonds...Just Bonds

Bonds are loans made to governments or corporations; they belong to the family of debt instruments. When you buy a bond, you're acting as the bank, collecting interest on the loan. At the end of the loan term, you get the full principal back, as long as you're the one holding the bond.

Just like people, bond issues come with credit ratings that highlight their credit risk, the chance that the issuer will default (not pay) when the bond matures or may miss scheduled interest payments. Bonds rated AAA have the lowest default risk. Bonds rated C or D are considered high risk and likely to default. There's an alphabet of ratings in between, but generally any bond rated BBB- or higher is considered "investment grade" (meaning safe). Bonds with noninvestment-grade ratings (lower than BBB-) are also called junk bonds. Just as people with good credit get lower interest rates, bonds with higher ratings pay less interest, and bonds with lower ratings pay much higher rates (this is why they're referred to as high-yield bonds).

HOW BONDS WORK

When you buy bonds from an issuer (the entity that creates the bonds), you're actually lending them money. In exchange, the issuer agrees to pay you interest on the loan and promises to pay back the principal on the bond's maturity date (the date the loan comes due).

Most bonds have face values (the principal that will be paid back) of $1,000, though that may not be the price you pay for the bond.

Bonds also trade on the open market, normally at a discount (less than) or premium (more than) to their face value. Whoever is holding the bond on the maturity date gets to collect the principal payoff.

The Secret Language of Bonds

Bonds come with their own vocabulary that sets them apart from other loans. Commonly used bond terms include:

- **Face value:** the amount of money (stated on the face of the bond) that will be paid back on the bond's maturity date and used to calculate the coupon payment
- **Issue price:** the amount of money the issuer sells the bond for, which usually does not equal its face value
- **Coupon rate:** the percentage of interest the bond issuer will pay on the bond's face value
- **Coupon payment:** the amount of interest in dollars that the bondholder will receive on each coupon date (for example, a 3 percent bond with $1,000 face value and semiannual coupon dates pays $15 per coupon payment for a total of $30 per year)
- **Coupon date:** the dates on which the issuer will make scheduled interest payments, usually semiannually
- **Maturity date:** the date the bond comes due and the full face value will be paid to the bondholder

These basic terms just scratch the surface of bond language. If you decide to delve deeper into the world of bond investing, make sure you understand all the terms and features of any bond you buy.

Discounts and Premiums

Bonds rarely sell for their face value. Instead, their prices depend on how their coupon rates compare to current interest rates. When prevailing interest rates are higher than the coupon rate, the bond will sell at a discount (less than its face value) or no one would want to buy it. The price difference forces the interest payment to equal what the market is paying. For example, if you had a $1,000 bond with a 3 percent coupon rate, you'd earn $30 per year in interest. If interest rates rose to 5 percent, that bond would sell for less than $1,000 in order to make the $30 interest payment work out to a 5 percent rate, or $600 ($30 / 0.05 = $600). The face value wouldn't change, but the effective interest earned on the $600 invested in the bond would reflect the 5 percent rate.

An investor would pay a premium (higher than face value) on a bond with a higher coupon rate than the current interest rate. So, if you had a $1,000 bond with a 5 percent coupon rate, and prevailing rates dropped to 4 percent, your bond would fetch more than $1,000 if you sold it. Premiums and discounts matter only when you're buying or selling bonds, not when you're holding on to them.

DIFFERENT TYPES OF BONDS

When you start investing in bonds, you'll see that there are dozens of options, but they all fall into two main categories: government and corporate. While the basic principles of both are the same, they do come with important differences that can dramatically affect the risks and returns in your portfolio. Which type you'll choose depends on the reason you want to add bonds to your holdings. If you're looking to reduce overall portfolio risk, government bonds can fill that role. If you want to earn higher-than-average interest rates and are willing to overlook some risk, consider corporate bonds. You can also go for a mix of fixed-income investments to add balance, income, and diversity to this piece of your portfolio.

Federal Government Bonds

The US government issues two main types of debt: Treasuries and savings bonds, and only Treasuries are used for straight investment purposes. The interest earned on these is exempt from state and local income taxes, but not from federal income taxes. These securities are considered to be risk-free, meaning there is no risk of default. Because of the zero-risk factor, US government debt securities have the lowest interest rates.

There are four types of Treasuries, and (technically) only two of those count as bonds. The four include:

- Treasury bills (a.k.a. T-bills), which have terms running from four weeks to one year and issue at a discount to face value (that discount equals the interest earned)
- Treasury notes, which mature in two to ten years and make semi-annual interest payments
- Treasury bonds (a.k.a. "long bonds"), which have maturities of at least ten years and pay interest every six months
- Treasury Inflation-Protected Securities (TIPS), which work like Treasury bonds with a twist—their face value changes based on inflation, so their coupon payments change as well

Municipal Bonds

States and local governments use municipal bonds (also called "munis") to raise money for public projects like fixing roads and building schools. The interest on municipal bonds is exempt from federal income taxes, which makes them a good choice to hold in nonretirement (regular) investment accounts. Plus, if you buy bonds issued by the state you live in, they'd normally also be state and local tax-exempt. Municipal bonds work best for people in higher income tax brackets, as the tax savings offset the lower interest rates they pay out.

Municipal bonds usually also come with a call feature, meaning the issuer can pay off the bonds before their maturity date. When a bond gets called, the issuer pays the bondholder the interest that's accumulated through that date along with the full call price (usually the face value) of the bond. Once a bond is called, bondholders will no longer receive interest income from that bond. You can buy munis through your bank or broker or directly from the state or local government office.

International Bonds

International bonds are debt securities issued by a foreign government or corporation in their native currency. Like other bonds, they come with scheduled interest payments and set maturity dates. These bonds come with extra risk based on their currency, which may change in value relative to US dollars.

Corporate Bonds

As the name spells out, corporate bonds are issued by corporations. These bonds typically come with higher (sometimes significantly higher) coupon rates than government bonds because they also come with more credit risk. Here, bond ratings matter much more than they do with government bonds, as companies are much more likely to default on their debts. Lower ratings come with higher interest rates to offset the extra risk.

In addition to the ratings, if you plan to buy and hold individual corporate bonds, look at the company's financial statements and financial position. Check to see whether the corporation generates enough income (its operating income) to cover its interest payments (interest expense). You'll also want to know whether the bonds are callable (the company can redeem them ahead of schedule) or convertible (where bonds can be exchanged for shares of corporate stock).

Since interest on corporate bonds is subject to federal, state, and local income taxes, many people hold these securities in retirement accounts. You can buy corporate bonds through your bank or broker.

MORTGAGE REITS

The Other Side of Home Loans

Mortgage real estate investment trusts (REITs) are sort of like mutual funds that invest only in mortgage debt. Some mortgage REITs act as direct mortgage lenders, while others buy up existing mortgages or invest in mortgage-backed securities (more on these in a second). Mortgage REITs primarily earn profits through the interest generated on the loans they hold (directly or indirectly).

When you own shares of mortgage REITs, you will own a portion of those underlying mortgage loans, and the interest income will flow (indirectly) to you. It gives you the main advantage of being a mortgage lender (interest income) without the risks inherent in making mortgage loans yourself.

What's a REIT?

Real estate investment trusts (REITs) are special investment funds with at least 75 percent of their holdings in physical real estate or mortgages. To qualify as a REIT, the fund must also receive at least 75 percent of its earnings from rents, profits from property sales, or mortgage interest and pay out at least 90 percent of those earnings to shareholders every year.

A CLOSER LOOK AT
MORTGAGE REITS

Mortgage REITs hold pools of mortgage loans and mortgage-backed securities, which are bonds backed by thousands of individual mortgage loans. These REITs earn income based on the interest portion of mortgage payments on the loans they hold. Mortgage REITs are considered to be risky investments because they only earn income when mortgage holders make their payments on time, neither late (going into default or foreclosure) nor early (like refinancing to a different loan or selling their properties). They're also sensitive to changes in interest rates, and may lose value when rates rise. To offset those risks, mortgage REITs often pay much higher dividends than similar types of investments (like property REITs).

What to Know Before You Invest

Like with any type of investment, it's important to understand the quirks specific to mortgage REITs before you buy shares. Two of the most important factors to look at when comparing mortgage REITs include leverage and spread.

"Leverage" refers to the portion of the REIT's holdings that are financed by debt (borrowing, meaning the REIT borrowed money to buy the mortgages it holds). When a REIT buys mortgages, it uses a combination of equity and debt to finance its purchases. The more equity it uses, the more profitable the REIT will be; less leverage is better.

"Spread" is the difference between the interest the REIT earns from its mortgage holdings and the interest it pays on debt. That difference, the spread, is the profit that will be passed through to shareholders. As you can imagine, bigger spreads are better for investors. REITs with more leverage will have smaller spreads.

You can learn more about mortgage REITs on the Nareit website at www.reit.com.

How to Invest in Mortgage REITs

Investing in mortgage REITs lets you bring real estate into your portfolio in a more flexible and cost-effective way than buying physical properties. It also lets you act as the lender, where you're on the profit side of debt.

There are currently (as of July 2019) twenty publicly traded mortgage REITs. You can buy REIT shares over major stock exchanges, just like you would buy shares of stock. You can also invest in mortgage REITs through mutual funds or exchange-traded funds (ETFs). You can find a comprehensive list of publicly traded mortgage REITs and information about each at www.reit.com.

RESIDENTIAL OR COMMERCIAL MORTGAGES?

Mortgage REITs cover both the commercial and residential real estate markets. Both types involve loans secured by land and buildings, but they work a little differently because residential mortgages have different features than commercial mortgages. Residential mortgages (the type most people are more familiar with) usually stretch over thirty years and have relatively high loan-to-value (LTV) ratios. Commercial mortgages, which cover properties like shopping malls and office buildings, usually have lower LTV ratios and shorter loan terms (twenty years or less) that end in balloon payments (giant payments due all at once).

The number of holdings in the REIT also varies widely between residential and commercial types. Residential mortgage REITs typically hold tens of thousands of home loans, either directly or through mortgage-backed securities. Commercial mortgage REITs usually hold fewer and much larger loans.

LTV Ratios

An LTV ratio compares the amount of a loan to the value of the corresponding property. For example, if a property was worth $500,000 and the mortgage on that property came to $250,000, the LTV ratio would be 50 percent ($250,000 / $500,000). Most residential mortgages have LTVs in the 5 to 20 percent range to start.

Commercial Mortgage REITs

Commercial mortgage REITs buy, issue, and invest in loans used to buy (or refinance) commercial real estate. Commercial real estate includes everything from self-storage facilities to cell phone towers to warehouses. Residential properties that have more than five units (like high-rise apartment buildings and college dorms) are usually included under the commercial umbrella. Mortgage REITs often hold a variety of commercial mortgages, but some may zero in on specific property types (like they only hold mortgages that cover medical facilities like hospitals and nursing homes).

Mortgages on commercial properties usually don't exceed twenty years, and most commonly last five to ten years. Although the loans are short term, payments are often calculated as if they were thirty-year loans, resulting in a balloon payment at the end. Commercial real estate loans also call for bigger down payments, requiring buyers to put up at least 20–35 percent of the property value. This reduces the lender's default risk—the risk that the borrower will stop making loan payments.

Residential Mortgage REITs

Residential mortgage REITs hold either pools of individual mortgage loans or mortgage-backed securities (MBSs), bonds backed by home mortgages. When borrowers make payments on these underlying mortgages, the REIT takes the interest portion as earnings. Those earnings get passed through to the shareholders.

Residential mortgage REITs face a lot of prepayment risk, the chance that mortgage holders will sell or refinance their properties; this happens much more often with residential loans than with commercial mortgages. That makes them riskier investments than commercial mortgage REITs.

Mortgage REITs that hold MBSs (rather than individual mortgages) normally hold bonds issued and backed by federal government-sponsored enterprises. Because of the federal connection, these MBSs come with less credit risk (the risk that mortgage holders will default on their loans) than individual mortgages or other types of MBSs.

PEER-TO-PEER LENDING

Cut Out the Middleman

Peer-to-peer (P2P) lending hit the debt scene in 2005 and has forever changed the way people borrow and lend money. For generations, banks and credit unions held the purse strings when it came to business and consumer loans. Now, with the explosion of P2P lending platforms, people all over the world engage in loan transactions completely outside the traditional banking world. That's opened up debt investing opportunities with the potential for much higher rates than you could get from other debt securities (such as bonds and bond funds). The promise of double-digit returns comes with some pretty steep risk, but with careful planning and loan selection, P2P investors can limit their downside risk and generate steady interest income.

GETTING STARTED WITH P2P

Investing in P2P lending seems easy, but that can be deceptive. The mechanics are simple, but choosing the right loans can be complicated and time consuming. If you're willing to put the work in, you can build a portfolio of profitable loans and earn more interest than you could in a bank account or with investment-grade bonds. Without careful due diligence, though, you could end up losing the whole pot.

Setting up an account on a P2P platform is quick and easy. Once you've chosen a lending platform (more on that in a moment), all you have to do is provide basic information to open your account (either regular or retirement) and then fund it. After you're set up, you can start reviewing potential borrowers and deciding who you want to lend money to.

Vetting Borrowers

No matter which lending platform you choose, you'll find thousands of borrower profiles to sort through. You can sort them by criteria like the loan category (medical debt, debt consolidation, or small business loans, for example), total loan amount requested, and yield (the potential return on your investment). When you see a listing that interests you, click through to the borrower profile to get more details.

These profiles will look different on different platforms but contain the same basic information, which includes:

- The borrower's state
- Monthly loan payment
- Loan interest rate and term
- The loan servicing fee
- Loan rating/grade (an indication of risk level for the loan)
- Detailed credit information on the borrower

Borrowers with lower ratings pay higher interest rates, just like people with poor credit scores do. Poor ratings indicate a higher risk of default, meaning that there's a high probability that the loan won't be paid back in full and on time. However, even borrowers and loans with higher ratings come with default risk—none of these loans are guaranteed.

Lending Money

With P2P lending, you have the option to lend the full amount or just a portion of any loan listed; a single loan can have multiple lenders (investors). Full loan amounts typically run between $1,000 and $50,000. Borrowers don't start making payments until their loan has been fully funded, so it could take a while to start seeing cash flow in. Once payments begin, a portion of each flows through to the investors. You can either cash out those proceeds as they come in or reinvest them in other loans on the platform.

You can minimize your risk by funding small amounts (sometimes as small as $25) of a large number of loans and diversifying your loan portfolio. For maximum diversification, choose loans with different purposes, grades, and maturities. Be aware that P2P loans are not liquid investments, and your money will be tied up for the entire loan term.

P2P LENDING PLATFORMS

The two biggest (and best known) players are Prosper and LendingClub, but there are many more P2P platforms out there. If you'd rather go with a newer or lesser-known platform, make sure to do due diligence on the platform itself before you give them your money.

Prosper (www.prosper.com) launched the first P2P lending platform back in 2005 and has funded more than $13 billion in loans since. The site offers loans ranging from $2,000 to $40,000 with terms of three to five years. Loan rates start at 6.95 percent and go up to 35.99 percent. You can get started investing with Prosper for just $25.

LendingClub (www.lendingclub.com) came on the scene in 2007 and shot straight up the charts. This platform has facilitated more than $50 billion in loans, most of which are used to refinance other debt. LendingClub offers personal loans ranging from $1,000 to $40,000 with terms of three or five years and interest rates ranging from 6.95 percent to 35.98 percent. This site also offers small business loans of up to $500,000 with APRs ranging from 9.77 percent to 35.98 percent. LendingClub requires a $1,000 deposit to open an account, but allows $25 minimum investments.

Upstart (www.upstart.com) is one of the newer players on the block (started in 2014), but it's quickly gaining in popularity and has funded more than $4.1 billion in loans. What makes Upstart stand out from the crowd is its rating system, which goes beyond the usual credit report and income. The platform considers several other variables to predict not only the borrower's ability but also their personal likelihood of paying back the loan. That system has gotten them an 89 percent payback rate, one of the highest in the industry. Loan amounts range from $1,000 to $50,000 with three- or five-year terms and interest rates ranging from 4.75 percent to 35.99 percent. The platform is only open to accredited investors, and the minimum investment is $100.

Funding Circle (www.fundingcircle.com) focuses entirely on small business loans in the US and the UK. A creditworthy small business can borrow up to $500,000 with competitive interest rates. Funding Circle loans the money, then sells shares of the loans as fractional notes (like IOUs from the platform) to investors. The minimum deposit required to open an account is $25,000, and the minimum investment for any fractional note is $500.

P2P lenders are heavily regulated by the US Securities Exchange Commission (SEC) and state securities regulators. Be aware that P2P investing may not be available in all states. For example, Prosper doesn't accept lenders from seventeen states (including Maryland, Vermont, and New Jersey); LendingClub bars investors from five states. Platforms (like Upstart) that only accept accredited investors are available for investors in all states.

What's an Accredited Investor?

Accredited investors must have net worth greater than $1 million (not including their homes) or have earned at least $200,000 (or $300,000 for couples) in each of the past two years and reasonably expect to earn that much this year. Visit www.investor.gov for more information about accredited investors.

HARD MONEY LENDING (TRUST DEED INVESTING)

The Other Side of Real Estate Investing

Hard money lending (HML), private loans that finance real estate purchases, is not a casual investment. It requires a great amount of due diligence, strict adherence to federal and local lending laws, a strong sense of the local real estate market, and *a lot* of cash. The prevailing feature of hard money loans is speed; most close within three weeks, and many borrowers expect even faster turnaround times. Like every investment, HML comes with pros and cons. You can maximize the pros and minimize the cons by clearly defining your investment objectives, thoroughly understanding the industry, and getting the right kinds of help.

HML 101

HML involves lending your own money to a borrower and requiring real estate as collateral to secure the loan. These loans are most often used by house flippers (people who buy properties to fix them up and sell them quickly), but may also be used by people who intend to fix up and rent a property or by builders. Unlike other types of loans, the borrower's credit report takes a backseat; here, the property behind the deal is the main deciding factor for lenders to consider.

There's a lot of profit potential with these deals, but risk of loss can be huge if you don't take steps to protect your investment. One of the most crucial elements of success is the ability to assess properties and their potential and knowing when to walk away when they don't meet your standard.

The Basics

Hard money loans usually come with short terms, usually less than one year. Returns are typically much higher than they are on other debt securities because of the extra helping of risk, even though that's offset by the mortgage (your claim on the property). Plus, you get steady cash flow from your borrower without any of the hassles of dealing with the property yourself (like you would if you were a landlord).

To navigate HML successfully you need a solid team, which will include:

* A real estate attorney familiar with lending laws
* A real estate broker
* An escrow company
* A loan servicing company (optional)

It's also helpful to connect with a local real estate investment club whose members regularly use hard money loans to finance their property purchases.

You'll want to develop your own lending criteria (much the way a bank would) to help you identify borrowers you want to work with. That could include things like the borrower's experience level with house flipping (people with a record of at least four successful flips, for example), down payment sources (the cash must come only from the borrower's savings, for example), and credit report. You'll also want to personally inspect the property to see if you agree with the borrower's assessment of its potential worth.

Know the Law

Before you lend any money, familiarize yourself with both the lending and foreclosure laws governing your deal. You need to fully understand any US Securities Exchange Commission requirements as well as state and local statutes. Make sure you look into state usury laws (more than half have them), which regulate maximum allowable interest rates; if you inadvertently charge a usurious interest rate, you may not be able to enforce collection of delinquent debts or foreclose on the property. Foreclosure laws may also call for specific steps that must be followed in order for you to claim the property in the event of a default.

Not the Same Thing

The terms "private money lender" and "hard money lender" are often used interchangeably, but they don't mean the same thing. While both describe private loans (rather than institutional loans), hard money lenders require "hard" assets (usually real estate) as collateral, and private money lenders don't.

Run the Numbers

Most successful HML insists on LTV (loan-to-value) ratios of no more than 70 percent of the after repair value (ARV) of the property. That means you expect the borrower to come up with at least 30 percent of the ARV as a down payment. Here's an example of how that would work. Say the borrower found a property selling for $100,000 that needs a lot of repairs. After making those repairs, the home could sell for $130,000 (its ARV). You would lend no more than $91,000 ($130,000 × 0.70).

You also want to make sure that you're not lending more than you would pay for the property as is. If that's less than the 70 percent, it might make sense to cap the loan at that value. Finally, don't forget to take into account the potential costs of foreclosure, including court costs and carrying costs (expenses between the time to claim the property and sell it).

AVOID COSTLY MISTAKES

Novice hard money lenders can end up decimating their wealth by making common, very expensive mistakes. These loans are usually quite large, and total loss can be financially devastating. You can take steps to avoid these errors and help increase your profitability potential. The most important: Do a lot of research and connect with experienced professionals before you make a single hard money loan.

This Is a Business

HML is a business as much as it is an investment. For your protection, consult a lawyer about the most advantageous business structure that can protect your personal assets from claims and lawsuits related to your HML business.

Get All the Proper Documents
HML comes with a lot of paperwork, and it's easy for documents to slip through the cracks. These documents help protect you against sizable losses. Make sure you have all of them (that apply to your

loan), and that each is properly signed and dated (and notarized, if necessary). Critical documents include:

- Promissory note, which serves as the primary loan document
- Mortgage, which secures your claim on the property
- Title insurance
- Proof of funds, to trace the borrower's down payment (bank or retirement account statements, for example)
- Proof of appropriate insurance and work permits
- Purchase and sale (P&S) agreement, which details the final sale terms for the property
- Independent appraisal reports for both before and after the property is rehabbed
- Home inspection report

Secure Title Insurance

Title insurance protects someone buying property against undiscovered liens (legal claims) against that property. Even after an extensive title search that seems thorough, unrecognized claims can (and do) crop up. When that happens, the preexisting claim takes precedence, and you and your borrower can lose your claims on the property. That's the purpose of title insurance, to protect against losses in that circumstance. However, if you are not named on the title insurance, you will not be covered. Make sure that you are explicitly named on the title insurance policy purchased by the borrower.

Don't Over-Invest in HML

Before you get started in HML, figure out how it will fit into your overall investing strategy. Depending on how you've labeled your asset allocation, hard money loans can count as debt, fixed income, or real estate investments in your portfolio. To keep your portfolio in the balance you want, swap out investments in that same category that are bringing lower returns, but don't overdo the risk factor if this is your safety section.

In addition, since HML requires large cash infusions, make sure you have enough liquid assets available to cover any need that might crop up (unexpected medical costs or major home repairs, for example). You also don't want to lend more than a set percentage of your total net worth (not including your home); for example, cap your HML portfolio at 10 percent of your net worth, an amount that's recoverable (in time) in the event of loss.

INDEX

ABOUT THE AUTHOR

Michele Cagan is a CPA, author, and financial mentor. With more than twenty years of experience, she offers unique insights into personal financial planning, from breaking out of debt and minimizing taxes to maximizing income and building wealth. Michele has written numerous articles and books about personal finance, investing, and accounting, including *The Infographic Guide to Personal Finance*, *Investing 101*, *Budgeting 101*, *Real Estate Investing 101*, *Stock Market 101*, and *Financial Words You Should Know*. In addition to her financial know-how, Michele has a not-so-secret love of painting, Star Wars, and chocolate. She lives in Maryland with her son, dogs, cats, and koi. Get more financial guidance from Michele by visiting SingleMomCPA.com.

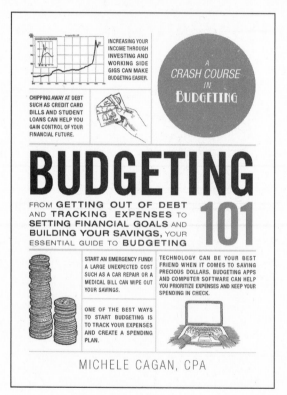